TBI – To Be Injured

*Surviving and Thriving
After a Brain Injury*

CAROL GIEG

ARCHWAY
PUBLISHING

Archway Publishing books may be ordered through booksellers or by contacting:

Archway Publishing
1663 Liberty Drive
Bloomington, IN 47403
www.archwaypublishing.com
1 (888) 242-5904

Because of the dynamic nature of the Internet, any web addresses or links contained in this book may have changed since publication and may no longer be valid. The views expressed in this work are solely those of the author and do not necessarily reflect the views of the publisher, and the publisher hereby disclaims any responsibility for them.

Any people depicted in stock imagery provided by Thinkstock are models, and such images are being used for illustrative purposes only. Certain stock imagery © Thinkstock.

ISBN: 978-1-4808-3780-5 (sc)
ISBN: 978-1-4808-3781-2 (e)

Library of Congress Control Number: 2016916310

Print information available on the last page.

Archway Publishing rev. date: 12/29/2016

AUTHOR'S NOTE

When I have used the pronoun, "you," herein, I am speaking directly to the reader, as though he/she were a comrade who has suffered a traumatic injury to the brain.

A pseudonym has been used for my neurosurgeon, about whom I think often, with deepest appreciation and respect for his masterful skills in the art of neurosurgery.

Lastly, please do not allow any typos or grammatical errors found herein, to distract you from the purpose of the book.

Gratitude

First, I want to express thanks to Stephanie Frame and Gwen Ash, my proverbial "cogs in the publishing wheel," for their patience and encouragement throughout the process.

I salute those working at the Rincon Valley library in Santa Rosa for putting up with my constant presence. Sometimes, being with others not knowing my circumstances and tolerating questions, contributed to my impetus to write. And hats off to "Irv," also a "frequent flyer" at the library, for his sense of humor and for informing me of where I could find free internet on days when the library was closed.

And thanks to those who understood without having to ask, and to those who wanted to learn from my experience. Thanks to Merry and Lisa for their priceless contribution to the title.

Finally, and most important, my deepest thanks, to all of my supportive friends and family, to my neurosurgeon, to my loving husband Luis, and to G-d, for giving me a life, now full and rewarding, once again.

PROLOGUE

TBI does not mean you are forever and only "someone who had a traumatic brain injury." You are a unique person, capable of change. You know from experience, what it's like To Be Injured (--a more accurate and positive translation for "TBI.") Do not accept that you can no longer accomplish what you once did without thought. Over the years, in my practice as a therapist, I've told many patients who've had strokes or other damage done to their brains, that they must give themselves time to adjust. The answers will re-emerge. If you are willing to work hard, to believe in yourself and the research supporting your abilities, there is no limit to what you can achieve.

Hopefully, those of you who have suffered a brain injury, will be blessed, as I have, with that most essential of ingredients-- family (both biological and the chosen kind) and friends, whose love, easily and unconditionally given, buoyed me to recover much of what I thought I'd lost forever. Do not accept that you're deficient, and seek out those who feel your pain with you. The progress you will make depends on it.

Hope can be restored, and fear released. Compassion for others and a desire to lighten their load, are the final destination in recovery from trauma.

Having reached this conclusion, I offer this hope to others. These reflections, this story, is my attempt to do just that.

INTRODUCTION

When someone dies, those left behind grieve. When we lose someone we love, someone we hold dear, the response of others is usually quick to comfort and support us in our loss.

The five stages of grief were first recognized by Elizabeth Kubler Ross in her seminal work, <u>On Death and Dying</u> (New York The MacMillan Company, 1969). These stages include denial, anger, bargaining, depression and acceptance. Those in the mental health field respect and study her work to this day, often employing it in the treatment of their patients.

Loss of cognitive capabilities, however, is not the same type of loss.

Having suffered injury to the brain, there are those of us who pass through some of these stages, but often through a few different ones as well. Movement back and forth between stages is common. The chance of remaining in one stage far longer than is beneficial, can happen when more emotional damage is done after the initial injury.

As I've experienced them, I suggest that a more accurate description of these stages would be: confusion, denial, anger, fear, and concluding in either despair or hope.

Acceptance is simply not part of the equation. Certainly it is important to accept that some things have changed. But, acceptance could be (and often is) interpreted as: "The possibility for improvement does not exist." The victim is condemned to live a life devoid of hope for any positive change, thus extinguishing any motivation to try. Those in despair have adopted limitations based on others' expectations.

Hope (fostered by support from others) springs eternal in those of us not relegated to such limits. It has allowed me to achieve a much enriched life. Only in this way was I able to share with other victims what I had experienced and accomplished. "Choosing," rather than "accepting" has made all the difference.

I cannot say if this is true for all who have been injured, but it has been so for me and others I know. Each of us will come to our own conclusions about who we are after being injured. I hope it is worthwhile to consider, and perhaps relate enough, not to fall into the abyss of despair.

There were several types of people in my world after being injured. Learning to recognize the differences between them facilitated my recovery. Some were, and still are, unconditionally supportive. They respected me and asked what I thought was best before applauding my efforts and considered solutions along with me. Their support allowed me to retain what I could, to recover much of what I'd lost, and to choose the adaptations I would need to make in order to live, once again, a fulfilling life.

Unfortunately, there were also those few who were not supportive, who, in fact, seemed determined that I should fail. It took a while to acknowledge (though never condone) that such behavior was immutable.

Remember, "No one can make you feel inferior without your consent." (Eleanor Roosevelt)

Another group of people I encountered pitied me, were sympathetic and usually meant to support me, to join in my recovery. Unbeknownst to them, if this went on too long, I felt hopeless, disempowered and even dependent. However, once recognizing the basis for their actions, I could make the choice to respond by acknowledging their intention, and be grateful that they cared.

Still others responded out of honest curiosity. These included those seeking something to put their troubled minds at rest, something they thought I would know because I had been so close to death.

Some were interested because of their desire to help others. People such as this were usually in the medical field and it is due to their knowledge and research, that so much has been accomplished over the past 20 years regarding what is known as TBI (Traumatic Brain Injury). I have such compassion for those who suffered a brain injury years before this. They spent many years without knowing what modern research has revealed since then.

Recently, much attention in the media has been given to the causes of traumatic brain injury, as well as to the harm that can be done to both children and adults. Here is a brief overview of what my search for information revealed:

"Brain injury is a major cause of disability in the United States, contributing to about 30% of all injury deaths... Every day, 138 people in United States die from injuries that include TBI...

Most TBIs that occur each year are mild, commonly called concussions...

In 2010, 2.5 million emergency department (ED) visits, hospitalizations, or deaths were associated with TBI--either alone or in combination with other injuries-- in the United States.

TBI contributed to the deaths of more than 50,000 people...TBI was a diagnosis in 280,000 hospitalizations and 2.2 million ED visits." (National Center for Injury Prevention and Control, 2010)

Specific focus on "mild traumatic brain injury" (concussion) as a result of different athletic activities which involve impact to the head, has even more recently been reported in the mass media. These activities include injuries which occur while engaging in sports (either professionally, or for recreation) such as football, soccer, and more....

A concussion, also known as a mild traumatic brain injury (MTBI), is caused by a bump, blow, or jolt to either the head or the body that causes the brain to move rapidly inside the skull. A concussion changes how the brain normally functions. Concussions can have serious and long-term health effects, and even a seemingly mild 'ding' or a bump on the head can be serious. Signs and symptoms of a concussion include headache, nausea, fatigue, confusion or memory problems, sleep disturbances, or mood changes; symptoms are typically noticed right after the injury, but some might not be recognized until days or weeks later.

How many sports related concussions occur each year?

An estimated 1.6-3.8 million sports and recreation related concussions occur in the United States each year. Between 2001-2005, children and youth ages 5-18 years old accounted for 2.4 million sports-related emergency department (ED) visits annually, of which 6% (135,000) involved a concussion.

In what sports are concussions most often reported?

In organized high school sports, concussions occur more often in competitive sports, with football accounting for more than 60% of concussions. For males, the leading cause of high school sports concussion is football; for females the leading cause of high school sports concussion is soccer.

Among children and youth ages 5-18 years old, the five leading sports or recreational activities which account for concussions include: bicycling, football, basketball, playground activities, and soccer.

Concussion & Brain Injury Facts

According to CDC estimates, 1.6-3.8 million sports and recreation related concussions occur each year in the U.S.

10% of all contact sport athletes sustain concussions yearly.

Brain injuries cause more deaths than any other sports injury. In football, brain injuries account for 65% to 95% of all fatalities. Football injuries associated with the brain occur at the rate of one in every 5.5 games. In any given season, 10% of all college players and 20% of all high school players sustain brain injuries.

87% of professional boxers have sustained a brain injury.

5% of soccer players sustain brain injuries as a result of their sport.

The head is involved in more baseball injuries than any other body part. Almost half of the injuries involve a child's head, face, mouth or eyes.

An athlete who sustains concussion is 4-6 times more likely to sustain a second concussion.

The effects of a concussion are cumulative in athletes who return to play prior to complete recovery.

Up to 86% of athletes that suffer a concussion will experience Post-Traumatic Migraine or some other type of headache pain. In fact, recent evidence indicates that presence and severity of headache symptoms may be a very significant indicator of severity of head injury and help guide return to play decisions.

1.5 million Americans suffer from traumatic brain injuries.

A traumatic brain injury occurs every 15 seconds.

Traumatic brain injury is the number one cause of death in children and young adults.

Traumatic brain injuries cause 1.5 times more deaths than AIDS

(Brain Injury Research Institute, 2016)

Because more and more studies have been devoted to this problem, our awareness is growing about brain injury.

Some of the impetus for research stems, no doubt, from the fact that many in my generation, the so-called, "Baby Boomers", are living longer. Thus, there will likely be more who develop dementia. So many more of us will become cognitively impaired in the years to come, with no hope of recovery or acceptable quality of life, if we cease exploring possibilities.

As Norman Doidge, M.D., a psychiatrist and psychoanalyst, explains (in the introduction to his book, <u>The Brain That Changes Itself</u>) "For four hundred years, mainstream medicine and science believed that brain anatomy was fixed. The common wisdom was that after childhood, the brain changed only when it began the long process of decline, that when brain cells failed to develop properly, or were injured or died, they could not be replaced. Nor could the brain ever alter its structure and find a new way to function if part of it was damaged. The theory of the unchanging brain decreed that people who were born with brain or mental limitations, or who sustained brain damage, would be limited or damaged for life.

However, more recent research in the fields of Neurology and Neuroscience, has revealed that, contrary to previous beliefs about the brain, some loss of brain function due to injury, may not be permanent in all cases." (pp. xvii, xviii).

"Dr. Doidge addressed the issue of changes in the field as he continued his research. He explored and found to be true, the findings of "a band of brilliant scientists, frontiers of brain science, who, in the late 1960s and early 70s, made a series of unexpected discoveries. They showed that the brain changed its structure with each different activity, perfecting its circuits so that it was better suited to the task at hand. If certain 'parts' failed, then other parts could sometimes take over. The machine metaphor, of the brain as an organ with specialized parts, could not fully account for the changes the scientists were seeing. They began to call this fundamental brain property 'neuroplasticity'." (pp. xviii, xix)

The idea that brain cells can 'retire' and regenerate has been researched at the Mayo Clinic:

"Current research in neuroscience at the Mayo Clinic Center for Regenerative Medicine, continues to expand our knowledge about central nervous system neurons and "the brain as a changing organ, one capable of repairing itself through a number of means.

Brain plasticity, also known as neuroplasticity or cortical remapping, is a term that refers to the brain's ability to change and adapt as a result of experience. Up until the 1960s, researchers believed that changes in the brain could only take place during infancy and childhood. By early adulthood, it was believed that the brain's physical structure was permanent. Modern research has demonstrated that the brain continues to create new neural pathways and alter existing ones in order to adapt to new experiences, learn new information and create new memories.

History and Research on Brain Plasticity

Psychologist William James suggested that the brain was perhaps not as unchanging as previously believed way back in 1890. In his book The Principles of Psychology, he wrote, "Organic matter, especially nervous tissue, seems endowed with a very extraordinary degree of plasticity." However, this idea went largely ignored for many years.

In the 1920s, researcher Karl Lashley provided evidence of changes in the neural pathways of rhesus monkeys. By the 1960s, researchers began to explore cases in which older adults who had suffered massive strokes were able to regain functioning, demonstrating that the brain was much more malleable than previously believed. Modern researchers have also found evidence that the brain is able to rewire itself following damage.

How Does Brain Plasticity Work?

The human brain is composed of approximately 100 billion neurons. Early researchers believed that neurogenesis, or the creation of new neurons, stopped shortly after birth. Today, it is understood that the brain possesses the remarkable capacity to reorganize pathways, create new connections and, in some cases, even create new neurons.

According to the website Neuroscience for Kids, there are four key facts about neuroplasticity:

1. It can vary by age; while plasticity occurs throughout the lifetime, certain types of changes are more predominant during specific life ages.

2. It involves a variety of processes; plasticity is ongoing throughout life and involves brain cells other than neurons, including glial and vascular cells.

3. It can happen for two different reasons; as a result of learning, experience and memory formation, or as a result of damage to the brain.

4. Environment plays an essential role in the process, but genetics can also have an influence.

The first few years of a child's life are a time of rapid brain growth. At birth, every neuron in the cerebral cortex has an estimated 2,500 synapses; by age of three, this number has grown to a whopping 15,000 synapses per neuron.

The average adult, however, has about half that number of synapses. Why? Because as we gain new experiences, some connections are strengthened while others are eliminated. This process is known as synaptic pruning. Neurons that are used frequently develop stronger connections and those that are rarely or never used eventually die. By developing new connections and pruning away weak ones, the brain is able to adapt to the changing environment.

Types of Brain Plasticity

Functional Plasticity: Refers to the brain's ability to move functions from a damaged area of the brain to other undamaged areas.

Structural Plasticity: Refers to the brain's ability to actually change its physical structure as a result of learning."

(What is brain plasticity? by Kendra Cherry, 2014)

These findings buoyed my hopes for some recovery and challenged those who were bound to ideas long since changed.

David Snowdon's work, as principle investigator for the "Nun Study of Aging and Alzheimer's Disease," determined several variables which contribute to a decrease in the potential for contracting this awful disease and its impact on those we love. A group of nuns were found to develop dementia characteristics at a much lower rate than was found in the general population. Years of study revealed specific daily activities of these women, which seemed to lower the risk of developing Alzheimer's Disease.

They socialized with each other, meeting often to discuss current events and how they might contribute best in the modern world.

They were very active, doing physical labor in the care of their convent, scrubbing the stone floors vigorously while on hands and knees. They did yardwork and their own home maintenance as much as possible.

They did not smoke or drink alcohol, as did many people. These two factors alone, (both then and now) accounted for a myriad of health problems. Their diet was simple and, by most people's standards, healthy.

They were very emotionally supportive of each other, thus equipping themselves to manage stress well, both in their personal and the modern world.

They were engaged in spiritual growth through prayer, as a daily practice.

Snowdon's study has lead to numerous others, exploring the life conditions which seem to reduce the risk of developing Alzheimer's disease.

Dr. Ethelle G. Lord posted an article in the blog of the International Caregivers Association, entitled The Four Pillars of Prevention (July 24,2015). This article elaborated on the variables contributing to prevention. "These include physical and mental exercise, diet, stress management, and spiritual growth."

Thus, socializing, engaging in mind stimulating exercises, eating well, not smoking, drinking in moderation, eating a healthy diet and engaging in some form of spiritual practice are significant in predicting and influencing brain health and cognition later in life.

But, most important by far (when all other factors are considered) is, as you might guess--exercise. I intuited this last one, long before it was proven to be true in controlled studies.

We can learn, then, ways to incorporate what we now know, into our daily lives. These activities stimulate the brain. Some might be as simple as doing crossword puzzles or playing chess. More formally, there are exercises touted to enhance cognitive function and memory. Many of these are now readily available online (e.g., Lumosity, Posit Science). Some of these "brain games," have been challenged regarding the claim that they have a positive effect on brain functioning. However, if scores improve, injured people may feel more optimistic versus without hope. The idea of exercising the brain (like a muscle) to grow stronger, seems possible. If we remain informed about research regarding the validity of the claims, our choice to continue, or not, may be empowering.

Other resources available, come in book form (e.g., The Memory Bible by Gary Small M.D. and, A User's Guide to the Brain by Harvard medical school professor, John Ratey M.D. This second book preceded Ratey's next book, Go Wild, (co-authored with journalist John Manning). Go Wild emphasizes the importance of exercise even more elaborately than does A User's Guide to the Brain. Their assertions are based on findings determined through research, as noted in the book.

Www HelpGuide.org (the "primary project of HelpGuideOrg International, a nonprofit organization) lists "The Six Pillars of Alzheimer's Prevention," including: "Regular exercise, A healthy diet, Mental stimulation, Quality sleep, Stress management, An active social life."

Other studies have replicated these results, some adding other variables which seem to predict positive outcomes. These include writing with the nondominant hand (Keep Your Brain Alive:83 Neurobic Exercises to Help Prevent Memories Loss and Increase Mental Fitness by Lawrence Katz, Manning Rubin, David Suter) and learning a new language as an adult (Growth of Language-Related Brain Areas After Foreign Language Learning --as reported in NeuroImage October 2012, Volume 63--(by Johan Martensson,

Johan Erickkson, Nils Christian Bodammer, Magnus Lindgren, Mikael Johansson, Lars Nyberg, Martin Lovden).

As I practiced those things purported to be helpful, I was more hopeful. It was not as necessary to build a fortress of anger to defend against the marauders of disappointment and criticism meted out by some others and, in time, by me!

Hope and rejuvenated self confidence, allowed the walls which limited me, to collapse, without fear consuming me. Ultimately, I did not have to remain angry. There was an alternative to defending myself in this way. Confusion and fear lurking, I could choose not to despair, but to hope and strive in the face of adversity, to be strong merely through asserting and encouraging myself and by spending time with those who believed in me.

As a licensed clinical social worker, I have spent my entire career life listening to others' stories, then defining with patients what inhibits their progress toward feeling fulfilled. I hoped to serve as a guide in finding the answers lying within each one of them, to achieve a life filled with hope, satisfaction, and the wisdom that they have something of value to offer others.

CHAPTER 1

Injured

Other things may change us, but we start and end with the family.

Anthony Brandt

We have been gifted with the best of friends. They taught us about love and what is important.

(Anonymous)

Friends are the family we choose for ourselves.

Edna Buchanan

This is the first part of my story, but, since I was not aware of what was happening much of the time, I've relied upon those whose memories are still vivid after all these years.

One morning, I dropped Luis off at the refinery, where he worked.

"Have fun babe!" he yelled as I drove away.

"Sure thing! I'll call you later." I assured him.

I drove to a small parking lot across town and parked my car, ready to take a long bikeride and pick him up later in the day. We then planned to meet a friend who would fly us in his plane to Los Angeles for the weekend. (The flight in his plane, no doubt, would surely be the most exciting part of the trip!)

I unloaded the bike, saddled up, and began the ride. It was a beautiful sun-drenched morning. A cool breeze rippled waves of fresh air through the parched grasses of late summer, portending the rainy season to come. I pedaled uphill for a while, imagining my legs as pistons pumping fuel into my quads. I rode along a brief plateau before plummeting down the steep grade into the town of Crockett.

After passing some refineries, I continued on into Pinole Valley, then over to Briones Park.

I remember coming to an area called Pig Farm Hill (no idea why). That is where I was found by the ambulance which took me to the hospital.

Meanwhile, my husband was oblivious to my situation. Luis was riding around the refinery with his partner, looking for parts required to repair equipment used in the various "units" of the refinery, that morning.

Suddenly, "Luis Colina! Luis Colina, report to your supervisor immediately!" echoed the demand heard throughout the refinery over the radios that each man carried.

"No! I just know it's Carol!" He'd been trying to reach me all day, without success.

Two friends who heard the urgent message echoing throughout the refinery, ran with Luis to the office where their supervisor was on the phone.

Seeing Luis, he stopped and handed him the phone.

"Someone needs to talk to you!" he explained.

"Hello?" Luis asked.

It was my manager, Linda, at Kaiser hospital in Santa Rosa. The Emergency Room staff had found some identification on me, along with my business card. They'd called the hospital and were transferred to Linda.

"Luis, Carol's had an accident. They're rushing her to the emergency room at John Muir hospital. Get over there as fast as you can! It's really serious and they don't know if she'll make it!"

Luis dropped the phone and raced for the door. Just outside was his friend, Jeff Bauer, who came running when he heard the call.

"Jeff, I need your help. Carol's had an accident, and I've got to get to John Muir hospital!" Jeff could see that Luis was in no condition to drive.

"Of course. Come with me." They both raced for Jeff's car and threw themselves into it.

Jeff hit the gas, and barreled toward the front gate of the refinery. The guard at the gate had been warned that they were coming and waved them through as they gunned it for the highway.

"G-d, oh G-d, no!" Luis cried in anguish, as they sped up the ramp and flew down Highway 24.

"It's okay, it's okay, Luis. We'll get there in time. We will! "Jeff reassured him.

Luis was in agony, a single image flashing through his mind, over and over again. This was the vision of me flying off my bike and landing on the unyielding asphalt, twisted and bleeding where I lay, unconscious.

Tears welled up in his eyes and streamed down his face.

While Jeff drove, Luis called everyone we knew to give them the news. He called not only to inform them, but, also, to seek some comfort.

First, he called my parents and sisters.

My mother asked many questions through sobs, but Luis could do no more than tell her where I was before hanging up. When he called my father, his wife, Patty, answered. She explained that my dad was not home but that she would reach him. They would come as quickly as they could.

My sisters, stalwart mothers of my nine nephews and one niece, somehow quickly arranged for care of the younger kids and caught the next planes out for California.

Next, Luis called our closest friends, our "second family."

Austin is a gifted special education teacher in Albany, California, as any of the parents of his students will be the first to tell you. When he got the news, he quickly arranged for someone to take over the class, ran to his car and took off for Walnut Creek.

Luis then called Margie who already had heard from Austin. Her kids, Amaya and Mateo, were able to stay with neighbors. She called Laura, her wife, and they quickly drove together from Albany toward the highway. Unfortunately, she felt her car list to the left.

"Shit! Not now!" Normally, a flat tire was no big deal to Margie, but today was different. She pulled over, took out the jack, and changed the tire, to an ominous dirge, "What if we don't make it in time?!"

Mario and Marcia, also dear friends, arranged for someone to stay with their son and daughter, Daniel and Amy, then headed for the hospital from Santa Rosa.

Next, Luis called Steve Rich and Larry Lapsley, two doctors who worked with me at Kaiser and were dear friends.

"Steve, Carol's hurt, I think real bad. I don't know what to do!"

"Luis, do you want us to come?"

"Yes, oh G-d yes!"

"Hang on, we're on our way!" They informed Linda, who arranged for coverage of their afternoon patients, and they were on their way in a matter of minutes.

Luis called others in the Bay Area and in other parts of the country where we had friends. He reached out in the hope that someone would help make sense of what was, to him, an incomprehensible situation.

Nancy was my loyal walking buddy, for many years, when she had lived in Santa Rosa. She hailed John, her husband, and caught a plane from Idaho to Oakland.

He rang one of my dear friends from Pittsburgh, Pennsylvania, now living in Oakland. We'd gone to high school together and had stayed in touch.

"What?! But, where are you? Can we come?" Bob asked. He called his wife, Kim, in San Francisco, where she worked. She dropped what she was doing, flew home to collect Bob, and whisked to the hospital to join the others supporting Luis.

Jeff exited the highway and drove east on Ygnacio Valley Road, until they reached John Muir Hospital. Jeff barely had time to come to a stop at the emergency room before Luis threw open the door and hit the ground running. Jeff followed close behind, leaving the truck at the entrance.

"Where is she?! Where is she?!" Luis demanded of the nurse at the desk.

"Who are you looking for? What's her name?" asked the nurse.

"Carol, Carol Gieg!" he cried.

Others in the waiting room stared at him, temporarily diverted from their own crises, injuries, and fears.

Jeff explained, "He just got a call that she was in an accident and might not make it."

"Oh!" she said as she came around the desk and grabbed his arm. "Come with me, come with me. She's here." Her expression registered alarm, but her voice was firm and in control. She was, after all, an emergency room nurse, well versed in managing crisis situations.

She guided him away from the others, down the hall.

"Mr. Colina, she's badly hurt. We called the surgeon and he got here right away. He's here only certain days each month, but, fortunately, today was one of those days. He and his team are getting ready, right now, to take her into surgery."

"But," he stammered, "What do you mean? Where is she?! I need to see my wife. I need to see her!"

"You will, Mr. Colina, you will. We simply couldn't wait for you, even for another minute. We didn't have time."

"But," he implored, "where is she?!"

"Mr. Colina, please calm down. They're taking her in right now, so you won't be able to see her yet. I'm going to take you to the surgery waitingroom."

Jeff followed right behind.

Once there, she turned to him again, "Mr. Colina, Dr. Peterson is the best neurosurgeon in the Bay Area. If anyone can save her, he can, but you have to wait here."

She turned to Jeff, "Can you wait with him here?"

"Of course. Luis, you have to stay with me."

"I've got to go now. They'll let you know as soon as possible, what's happening." And with that, she headed back to the Emergency Room.

Luis scanned the room, his fervent expression speaking volumes to the others there. He was a tortured animal, trapped in a cage created by those who would keep him from me.

Jeff put his arm around Luis's shoulder and said, "Luis, it'll be okay. Come on. We're going to pray for her."

He drew Luis aside and bowed his head, "Dear Father, please be with Luis and his wife, Carol. Bless them with the comfort of your love and help him through this terrible time. In Jesus' name, amen." Jeff's simple words were like mortar to the precarious mound of rocks on which Luis struggled to stand.

A nurse returned and scanned the room, undeterred by the misery of those waiting. She was used to seeing people writhing in pain and despair.

Luis was at her side instantly and the nurse explained," Mr. Colina, she made it to the surgery room and they're operating on her now."

Over the next several hours, our closest friends joined Luis and Jeff in the waitingroom. They surrounded and soothed him as much as they were able.

Steve and Larry were ready to help in ways no one else could. They translated "medicalese" (the unique vernacular of the medical field) into layman's terms, so that Luis could fully understand.

My mother, Holly, appeared, took one look at Luis, and ran to him, "Luis, is she... How is she, honey?"

He couldn't answer at first, so she put her arms around him. He told her that I was alive and in surgery. Other friends came forward and gave her more details. Fortunately, they all knew her.

The hours passed as friends sat vigil with Luis all afternoon and long into the night. The nurse appeared every few hours, to report on the progress of the surgery, to tell him I was still alive.

Margie and Austin volunteered to go and collect my car from the lot in Martinez. Austin avoided hospitals as a general rule and needed a break, though was embarrassed to find himself crying all the way there and while driving the car back.

"The thought of losing you rocked my world!" Austin explained later.

Once back at the hospital, they parked the car and returned to the waitingroom, now filling with our friends who had heard. Luis repeated to the others, over and over again, what little he'd been told about my condition. I'd been injured while riding, had seizures and bleeding in my brain, and was now in surgery. His composure returned, though tears flowed, the more he recounted the story.

Finally, after many more hours, the nurse appeared one last time, "Mr. Colina, the surgery is over and Dr. Peterson is coming to see you now."

Her words, like a stone thrown into a pond, rippled throughout the room. All eyes turned toward the doors leading into surgery, as Dr. Peterson emerged from its depths.

"Mr. Colina, Mr. Colina, let's talk over here." Jeff walked with the two of them, followed by Larry and Steve.

"Can they come too?" He pointed at Larry and Steve, it being a given that Jeff would join.

"They're doctors." Luis explained.

"Of course, "Dr. Peterson agreed.

Standing slightly apart from all, he began, "She's alive, Mr. Colina. She survived." He spoke to Luis directly, others within earshot.

"Thank you, thank you, doctor!" Luis's hands clasped together, as though in prayer.

As others in the room registered the look on Luis's face, each person embraced the one closest to them.

Dr. Peterson then described to Luis, in some detail, all that was done in surgery.

"She suffered a severe blow to the head when she fell. This caused a hematoma (a large swelling of blood) to form, causing pressure on her brain."

"Wha..?" choked Luis, and Jeff grabbed his arm to steady him.

Dr. Peterson continued, "We managed to relieve the pressure and the bleeding has stopped, but we won't know for days yet, whether or not she'll survive."

Luis moaned and Jeff interjected, "Luis, she's alive."

"She was in great shape prior to the injury, and her blood pressure was lower than expected throughout the surgery," the doctor said.

Luis explained, "Carol exercises all of the time, more than anyone I know. She doesn't like gyms. She hikes, bikes, or swims every day. She loves being outdoors."

"Oh, well that's surely one of the reasons she still alive," replied Dr. Peterson.

"Can I see her?" Luis asked, regaining his composure.

"No, not yet," Dr. Peterson replied, "We're going to have keep her here in recovery so that we can keep a close watch. She's still in a coma, but is recovering. She won't wake up for quite a while. It's really best for you to go home now. There's nothing more you can do tonight."

"But, but I want to see her," Luis begged, "When can I see her?"

"She's heavily sedated and we're monitoring her closely. The next few days are crucial and we don't want her stimulated too much."

"But," Luis stammered.

The surgeon continued, "We'll keep her here until she's stable. It's time for you to go home. You can come back in the morning and we'll know more. She won't wake up tonight."

"I'm going back in there now." He said, glancing toward at Steve and Larry. Once assured of their support, he departed. Assiduously avoiding the questioning stares of friends and family, he disappeared back through the double doors into his domain. Once there, he checked on me and instructed the others now responsible for my care. He repeated this procedure throughout the days that followed.

Luis stood silent, numb and in shock.

"Luis, it's alright, it's OK," Steve and Larry reassured him.

"But, what's still wrong? Why can't I see her?" Luis asked them.

The two doctors spent the next hour sitting with Luis, translating what had happened and what likely lay ahead. They repeated that I would not be conscious for quite a while, that it was amazing I'd survived at all. Luis wanted to know more, seeking the certainty they could not give, yet relishing the fact that I was alive, that he would see me again.

Mixed tears and smiles peppered the waitingroom, as Luis returned. As he repeated the news to them, they responded wholeheartedly, hugging and holding him close once again. They consoled and urged him to take the doctor's advice and head for home. It was 2 AM by then, and some had long journeys to travel. Gradually, most departed, but many chose to return the next day and repeatedly told Luis that they were ready to do whatever they could, whenever he needed them. But, he refused to budge. Finally, only Marcia, Mario, Steve and Larry remained. The doctors finally convinced him to go by reminding him that Dr. Peterson wanted me to be stimulated as little as possible in order to recover. I would remain unconscious for quite a while, after all. Finally, he agreed to leave.

It was then that Marcia, in her own inimitable fashion, took over.

"Come on Luis," Marcia said, putting your arm around him and drawing him toward Larry and Steve. They agreed to take Luis home, as no one felt comfortable with him driving alone. He'd been up since 4 o'clock that morning when he'd left for work.

Marcia continued, "Mario will drive your truck." She stated this as a fact, not a question. "He'll stay with you tonight and bring you back in the morning."

Luis knew, by the tone of her voice, that there was no choice in the matter.

Steve and Larry stepped forward, "Come on Luis. You're going with us," as they shepherded him to their car.

Once inside, he finally broke down, "Oh! Why Carol? Why her?!" He held his head in his hands and rocked slowly back-and-forth.

When they reached the house, Mario was already there waiting.

After Steve and Larry left, Mario put his arm around Luis, who shuddered and burrowed into the couch cushions

"It's going to be alright, Luis. It's going to be alright." Mario comforted.

"Oh, Mario! What if it was me?"

"What do you mean?" Mario asked.

Luis started to cry again, "I take care of her bike. What if I forgot something? What if it's my fault?!"

"No, Luis, no. Someone hit her. It wasn't your fault."

Mario stayed all night. He was worried, as were Marcia and the others, about what Luis might do if he were left alone.

That concern was soon resolved. Our friends Gina and Bill, opened their door and hearts and allowed Luis to stay in Benicia, (a town nearby) as much as he needed during my hospitalization. They lived not far from the hospital, gave him his own key and helped him to process his feelings as I progressed. He was never without someone to lean on.

CHAPTER 2
Day 2

I get by with a little help from my friends.

The Beatles

Early the next morning, Luis was back in his truck and on the way to John Muir. Jeff was already there, waiting for him, when he arrived. Together, they sat in the now familiar hospital waitingroom, a haven for those in a holding pattern, as the hands of the large white analog clock on the wall ticked off the interminable seconds, minutes, hours and days.

As the morning wore on, others arrived, including some from the refinery. Laura (a good friend and employee at Kaiser) returned, as she did every day thereafter, an integral disc in the backbone of support. She was particularly intuitive that morning.

One look at Luis's face and she knew something had changed. His haggard countenance attested to the sleepless night spent tossing and turning, nightmares littering his dream world, like landmines, secreted and deadly. She noted the furrows deepening around his eyes and brow, following the torrential storm of tears the day before. He seemed even more removed, intensely focused on what, she could not see.

"Luis, what happened since yesterday? What is it? "she asked.

He didn't answer at first. She stood by and waited. Finally, he said, "It could've been my fault, her bike. I'm the one who fixes it. What if I missed something?"

Laura tried to reason with him, just as had Mario the evening before. Still, it was curious. I was a seasoned rider, well acquainted with the route from Martinez to Crockett, through Rodeo into Briones Park, over Pig Farm Hill, and back into Martinez. I had ridden that route many times, so the conclusion that I had simply "fallen off," (as the police report indicated) seemed ludicrous, at best.

Eventually, since nothing seemed to convince him, Luis decided he should go pick up my bike at the police station.

"I'll go with you," Laura suggested.

He readily accepted the offer and they drove to the police station. When they arrived, they managed to speak with the same policeman who was actually on the scene the day before. Luis collected the bike and tenderly settled it into the truck bed. He was surprised to see that, "Caroleena," (his name for my bike) was virtually unscathed.

The officer offered to take them to where he found my body, on Pig Farm Hill, a desolate area of rolling sunburnt hills. He explained, again, that I had simply fallen off my bike, and they had no witnesses.

Luis's shoulders bowed forward, as his chin dropped to his chest.

Seconds later, he rallied, took a deep breath, and said, "Right. Let's go."

Laura could virtually see the wheels as they turned in his head, intensely focused and driven toward his goal.

When they arrived at the exact location, Luis inspected the area. I had been coming down the hill in the right-hand lane. Roadwork was being done on the left. No one from the crew had called for help when the injury occurred, so it was not likely they were working there that day.

Laura watched as Luis took measurements, seemingly from every angle, as he walked up and down the hill. Finally satisfied with the data, he squatted on his heels and busily scratched a diagram on the ground, which he later would assess and transfer to paper. My water bottle was twenty feet above where the report said I was hit, so it was not likely that I simply "fell" off my bike.

Suddenly remembering Laura, he returned to the car where she waited.

"Hey Laura, sorry this is taking so long."

"Oh, that's okay Luis! Take as long as you want." She got out of the car and began walking around, just to help him feel more comfortable.

"What did you find out, Luis?" she asked. She could see that he was more relaxed.

"Well, based on where her helmet and water bottle fell, and taking into account that it was straight downhill over the edge, there's no 'friggin way she just fell! Somebody hit her!"

"Okay, Luis, okay. "Laura said, as she watched the fear and helplessness on his face dissolve into anger. This was a much safer place for Luis to be.

Luis turned toward the policeman, "No way she just fell off there."

But the officer insisted, "Yes, that's where we found her."

"But look up there. Her water bottle is 20 feet up the hill, and she was right by the side of the road. Her bike is barely scratched."

The officer, even given his desire for it to be as stated in the report, had to admit that Luis was right. Somewhat mollified, Luis returned to the hospital, a hopeful expression replacing the pained one he'd worn earlier.

By the time they got back, the waitingroom was filling again with wellwishers for Luis and I. Some had returned from the day before. Others arrived for the first time, each contributing to the effort in their own unique way.

The nurse approached Luis and said, "Mr. Colina, she is just beginning to show signs of consciousness, and we wanted you to be with her, if she wakes up. We need to know if she can recognize you, if she can hear and register what's happening."

Luis was gone for a long time and returned to see me as often as was allowed in the days that followed. I was not fully awake for some time, though I showed some response to him initially.

Once I was more stable and awake, family and closest friends were allowed visits as well.

"Wow," was all Margie could muster when she first saw me in bed, my body covered entirely by a sheet. There was nothing recognizable as me, except for my eyes, nose and mouth which were encircled by swaths of bandages wrapped thickly around my head. Intravenous lines and monitors surrounded the bed, pumping and pulsing in unison, the very rhythm of my life.

"Carol, Carol! Hi, it's me, me and Margie!" Laura beamed. I must have looked confused.

"I don't think she recognizes us." Austin choked.

The nurses reassured him. They were disappointed, though not entirely surprised.

"Dr. Peterson said that she might not recognize your face, maybe for days. But that's OK, she probably will soon."

Margie tried to better prepare friends and family, after talking with Luis to Dr. Peterson. Steve's wife, Esther, came with him that day. Esther was a member of my book club, and another dear friend.

There was one visitor, however, who was neither family, nor friend. She asked questions at the desk, but, once she was told I was going to make it, she left, and was never seen again. Later, after I returned home, I met with someone who investigates such things, if only to see who she was.

I thought she might have been the one who hit me. It was a woman who had called 911.

He concluded it was not worth pursuing, which was fine in the end. After more thought, I decided, "What good would it do anyway?" I wouldn't feel better physically, no matter what the outcome.

She would have to live for the rest of her life with what she did, and I would only be angrier. The outcome from then on would be no different, so why waste the energy?

Kim and Bob Egan stopped by Market Hall to stock up on delicious morsels and deli delights, spreading them liberally throughout the room at lunchtime. Kim was the CEO of a company involved in creating delicious foods for large fine restaurants and businesses. Being well-schooled in the culinary arts, she was astutely conscious of the soothing and refreshing aspects of food. When cooking a meal to share, she, like Luis, was giving a gift to their guests.

As predicted, the food shared amongst fiends, served to loosen tongues and to help all of them focus on something other than fear and distress.

Marcia and Margie put their heads together. Despite offers, Luis had not eaten and others in the waitingroom had eaten little. Most had not thought to bring food initially, had not anticipated the length of time they would be waiting.

"How are we going to be sure he eats?" asked Marcia.

"Don't know, but we have to think of something. "agreed Margie.

They decided to create a list of people assigned to bring food on specific days. Soon, the list was completed for that first week. Through providing meals, our friends felt less demoralized and helpless.

Eventually, and as quickly as possible, my father, his wife and my sisters, arrived from across the country. They exchanged greetings, shared details, and gradually managed, somehow, to move on from mortality issues and vulnerability to happier memories. Such is human nature at its most resilient.

Since so much was unfathomable, so little predictable, minds and mouths grew less inhibited. The tension in the room was palpable, leading people to say things which, in retrospect, made little sense. This served, though inadvertently, to divert attention through providing some humor to an otherwise grim situation.

"You know how I finally got rid of 'em?" Austin asked those who expressed an interest in his successful battle with troublesome skunks and their nauseating spray.

"You'll never guess--tomato juice!" Having completed the tale, he giggled nervously, "Where did that come from?!"

Never mind, laughter permeated the room! The tale distracted and was just "what the doctor ordered," so to speak! Life was moving forward (though with regular schedules temporarily on hold) for Luis and those who loved us.

Luis looked across the room at one point, and spied my dad (hard to miss, all 6 foot 6 of him) having what appeared to be, a very serious conversation with Luis's boss, Dale Peterson.

"Ha!" chuckled my Dad in that inimitable chortle which Luis so ambitiously tried to perfect. After a time, Dale went back to the refinery and my father approached Luis.

"Hey, Luis, your boss is one helluva good guy! And he sure thinks the world of you. He told me so himself! I told him that was no surprise. After all, that's my son-in-law he was talking about!"

Luis knew that my father raised me infused with the persistence and determination I so needed at the time. He smiled, possibly for the first time since the day before. Luis was proud of his work, but especially when acknowledged by someone he so respected.

Here again, a moment of kindness, of good humor, provided the support so essential during those first few days. Life was moving forward. I was going to be alright, thanks in no small part, to these steadfast and loving people.

CHAPTER 3
CarePages

Hospital Waiting Rooms

"Where tears fall with abandon but the cries of joy
and thanksgiving mean more than we can imagine."
Communicating.Across.Boundaries

Once stabilized and moved to Kaiser's rehabilitation site, I began the long and often arduous road to recovery. People did not notice how difficult it was at first and, in fact, were surprised at how well I functioned. Luis began having difficulties as the number of calls increased.

"I know everyone's interested and it feels good. But, I feel guilty that I can't get back to everyone. It's just too much!" Luis complained to Margie.

"Don't worry Luis. I'll handle it," Margie said, and she did.

Margie "took the bull by the horns" and created a blog built to update those interested, on my progress. This solved the problem and reduced the number of calls and requests for information from Luis. Those at work and elsewhere could follow my experiences and progress. I have no doubt that words, thoughts and prayers contributed significantly to my recovery.

The first entry:

"Dear friends,

You are aware by now that our Carol was in a serious bike accident on Thursday, September 28. Luis has asked me to start this Carepage as a means of helping Carol's wonderfully supportive family and friends to stay informed and in touch about how she's doing. For now, I (Margie) will be posting daily updates. As he is able in the future, Luis may also send out the updates."

As you have all had varying levels of contact about Carol in recent days, I will try to briefly summarize the past few days for you. Carol was biking on the park road in Martinez on Thursday morning, September 28. She was thrown off her bike, causing a severe head injury and less serious collarbone fracture. A passerby called 911 and the ambulance arrived in time.

Carol was not conscious and was in very serious condition when she arrived at John Muir Hospital (one of the best trauma centers in the Bay Area, thank goodness!). She was placed on a respirator (intubated) had emergency brain surgery to deal with a hematoma, brain swelling\bruising, and right temporal lobe trauma. The doctor was very guarded in his hopes that evening. However, Carol remained stable through the night. On Friday morning, a brain scan showed that the swelling had stopped and there's just been one bit of positive news after another since that time!"

One of the responses following:

"Dear Carol and Luis – just a note to say you're in my thoughts and prayers. I know you are surrounded by the kindness and support of friends and family, a reflection of the way you both have touched the lives of others. I wish you strength for the journey ahead."

Later, Margie updated, "A few highlights… On Friday Carol was also moving her right and left sides intentionally in response to touch. On Saturday, Carol opened her eyes for the neurosurgeon and nodded yes when he asked if she could see him. She was also tracking movement with her eyes. The medical staff began tapering off of the ventilator and sedating medications. Late Saturday night, Carol (still intubated and with all sorts of tubes and monitors attached to her) sat up in bed and tried to get out of bed when the nurse left her alone for a minute. That's our Carol!!! Places to go, people to see! Today is Sunday. This morning, the doctors removed the ventilator and Carol spoke a few words!"

"Luis and Carol's family are grateful for all of your thoughts, prayers, and kind messages. Carol is still vulnerable and will remain in ICU for some time. Visits are limited to family members right now and, even then, visits only for short periods of time. Luis, of course, is now allowed longer visits and often needs to spend more time with Carol to reassure her and help her stay calm as she continues to 'wake up.' She clearly recognizes his voice and feels more peaceful when she knows he's there, even though she's mostly sleeping or semi-conscious at this point. She is still very exhausted and needs a tremendous amount of rest. There are still unknowns about her recovery, but we are all feeling so hopeful, knowing also that Carol is such a determined, strong, healthy, and amazing woman!"

"Please feel free to use the 'message board' for your well wishes and notes to Carol, Luis, and family/friends. I will make sure that the messages are delivered quickly to Luis until he is able to view them online himself. If you have any questions, you can post those as well or just email me. You can also send cards to Carol and Luis at their home address. Love to all, Margie."

Then, on October 2:

Dear friends,

"Another amazing day for Carol! She is awake and talking with Luis and her family! In contrast to previous days, the ICU staff are now encouraging Luis and family to visit with Carol and engage her with conversation. She has recognized everyone and seems to be following conversations, occasionally adding a comment herself. She is still pretty tired, nodding off frequently, and sometimes seems a little confused about things. The medical staff had to summon the physical therapist to evaluate Carol for mobility, since she was insisting on getting out of bed. She was given the green light to sit up in the chair next to her bed, and she seems to be satisfied with this...for now. She's still connected to a few tubes, but I am told that they may remove the feeding IV and let her start eating on her own after a speech therapist evaluates her swallowing ability soon."

Nancy (an avid hiker with me) and John, both friends from Idaho, had caught the first plane they could after Luis called them. They didn't know if they would arrive in time to congratulate me and Luis that I was still alive, or, to attend a funeral. Once Luis was given permission to allow others a chance to join me, Nancy did what no one else could have done as well.

Nancy began her visit by congratulating me on surviving, then immediately launched into an update on my surrogate son, Kenny, and a young woman in Nancy's life named Jackie.

"You're going to have to slow down a bit. She just had a brain injury, after all," Nancy was admonished by the nurse.

I looked her in the eye, as Nancy remembers it. Obviously annoyed, I said, "I can understand every word she says." And so, the conversation continued.

A few days later:

"Sorry for the late posting. I know you were all anxious to hear how Carol is doing. 105 friends and family have registered for this support page already and 35 loving messages have been posted. Send more! I will print out and take them to Luis tomorrow. He was so happy to hear about these responses. I think it makes the challenges of the day feel lighter, just knowing that so many people are thinking and caring about them!"

And another, this time devoted to comments made by well wishers:

"Margie – Your daily updates are really appreciated by the small group of Carol's 200 closest friends (!) It's a really good way for Carol and Luis to manage the huge interest in Carol's welfare and progress. Thank you."

"Carol – You've been such an inspiration to your friends and family for so long, why not just take it easy for a while and let others look after you?? You'll be 100% before long, and back to your old tricks, but it's OK to relax now and then!"

And this one, particularly poignant to me: "Dear Carol and Luis, you give new meaning to the words, 'One day at a time.' We are so happy to hear about your astounding daily progress. Luis, it is very touching to hear in the updates about your love for Carol and how you advocate for her. Like the way you made sure she got help with her pain level (and what a difference that made). We are sending our love."

"Luis – Carol is lucky to have such a devoted husband. Thanks from all of us for looking after her so tirelessly."

The October 3 entry was next:

"Lots to report on Carol today! Luis was with her until 1 AM last night because she was so restless and plotting her escape from the hospital. A tired night nurse informed Luis this morning that Carol tried to get up 21 times last night after he left. Carol is mostly oriented to reality in that she recognizes people, knows the date, and understands that she is in the hospital because of the bike accident. However, she sometimes gets confused and thinks that she needs to leave the hospital to get home or to work. Yesterday she was particularly worried about missing the breast cancer and bariatric support groups, which she facilitates at Kaiser. She is still in the process of 'waking up,' so, although she might talk and move about, you get the sense that she still is sleeping. She had a particularly sleepy day today, because they gave her morphine this morning to get her to sleep through the CT scan. The scan showed that her brain condition is "stable" and they are talking about possibly removing the final brain drain tube tomorrow. Good news that things are still steadily moving forward!"

Shortly thereafter:

"While I was at the hospital today, the neuropsychologist came to speak with Luis about her preliminary assessment of Carol. She says that it is still too early to predict the long term picture for Carol. She's definitely impressed with Carol's rapid recovery thus far and thinks that there are many very hopeful signs for Carol's recovery. Still, she made it clear that Carol will need intensive rehabilitation following acute hospitalization. Apparently Kaiser Vallejo has an excellent acute rehab program. Thanks go out to Carol's Kaiser friends/supports, who are already making connections necessary to assure that she will have the VIP treatment when the time comes for her to move to that hospital! I imagine it will still be a number of weeks before they even start talking about that sort of transfer.

The neuropsychologist did share an amusing anecdote with us… When she asked Carol if she knew the date, it was apparent to her that Carol was sick of being tested for orientation (the nurses do this hourly for head injury patients) so, instead of answering as usual, Carol used her fingers to indicate the series of numbers 10/3/2006! We enjoyed hearing of Carol's feisty and creative response!

On a note of equal importance, Luis wanted me to let you know that we ate dinner at Gordo's Gourmet Hamburgers at the shopping plaza to the east of the hospital. In honor of Carol's habit of striking up conversations with strangers, Luis befriended the proud restaurant owners and told them that we would be sending everyone to their newly-opened restaurant. We can vouch for the delicious burgers!

Carol's sisters left for their respective out-of-state homes today. All three sisters were able to visit with Carol together yesterday and she was well aware of their presence. I am so glad they were able to leave after actually seeing AND speaking with Carol! Carol's Dad and his wife, Pat, have extended their stay another day and will be leaving Thursday morning. Carol's mom, Holly, lives here in California, so she'll be spending time with Carol and Luis. Everyone seems to be holding up pretty well. I hope that you can imagine how wonderfully supportive they all feel when they read your Carepage messages. I delivered all 46 of the messages posted by noon today, but I can see that there are 84 messages and 186 people registered just 10 hours later! Luis says that he can feel the power of your prayers and healing energy being generated for Carol!

Good night, Margie"

Responses: "I miss seeing your smiling face, and all of us at Kaiser look forward to your return. My thoughts and prayers are with you."

And another, "You greatly influenced our lives by your words and you continue to inspire us by your actions. Our love to you and your family."

Shortly after:

"Today, she left the ICU. She's ambulatory but still pretty incoherent. She recognizes us but does not fully understand why she's in the hospital. She is, at times, obsessed with getting back to work. She's worried about missing a particular eating disorders group that she really likes to facilitate. We get to the point when we say, "OK, put on your sneakers, let's go to work", because she just won't let go of the idea. We walk her around the nursing station on our way to "work" until she becomes less focused on work and we can get her back to her room and direct her into another conversation."

Then, "She is already up and walking through the halls, driving the nurses crazy."

Response: "Carol, how awesome to hear of your continued, swift recovery! Your love shared with others has certainly brought Divine Favor your way! I look forward to your warm smile and twinkling eyes! Until then know that you and your loved ones are in my prayers! God bless!"

This one followed, with the thoughts of a dear friend: "One of the first things I do every morning is check in on you, Carol. I love to read all about your shenanigans and keep up on your progress. It was wonderful to get a first-hand report from Steve after his visit with you and Luis. I look forward so much to when you both come home and I want you to know that I will be there for you both. You can call on me anytime and I will be available to help in any way."

This entry is still particularly touching, even after all these years:

"Dear Carol, we have never met and will, likely, never meet.… I suffered a brain injury a little over a year ago. Thanks to a loving and devoted wife and much hard work, I am back at work my usual 50 to 60 hours every week and hope to soon resume scubadiving. Your wonderful spirit and drive to get better will serve you well in the ordeal you have only begun.

I will think of you often in the coming days and pray for continued and complete recovery."

One day, I walked with the help of a dear friend who had neurological challenges of her own. Because of this, she could relate to my situation better than others. Sensing acutely my desire and assessing my capability, she helped me walk briefly in the hallway before others arrived one morning. She is a doctor and knew I was physically capable, though would have likely been prevented if it were known that I was walking that far.

My husband, understandably, was a bit peeved at first, until he was told who it was that took me walking.

Once proven that I could do this, I was immediately allowed by the nursing staff, who cleared it with Dr. Peterson first.

During rehabilitation in hospital, I surprised even the physicians.

Because I made such rapid physical progress, many of those not in the medical field, expected that I would return to normal in every way. I wasn't aware, at the time, what I was expected to do in the aftermath of such an injury and surgery.

I was going to recover physically what I had lost, though this took place over time as I adapted and worked hard at it. That determination predicted my eventual return to full physical function.

But, cognitive capacity was still to be determined. Later, while at the Rehabilitation Center, I was given psychological testing by a trained professional.

Results revealed some changes in certain areas of the brain which were damaged when I was injured. I first recognized (though did not accept at that time) these changes during the exam. I had the most trouble with visual spatial reasoning and orientation, just as predicted by Dr. Peterson.

Surprisingly, my memory capacity, though not as good as before, fell within the average range. I was no longer at a superior level of cognition. This was the first time I realized how very intelligent I had been before.

Lesson one on the road to recovery: never, never take your memory, your mind, for granted. It is a gift and yours to guard, nourish, and exercise, should you want it to serve you longer and well.

CHAPTER 4
Childhood Injuries

Children are happy because they don't have a file in their minds called "All the Things That Could Go Wrong.

— Marianne Williamson

When I first awoke in the hospital, I was confused.

"Where am I? What's going on?"

The hospital setting didn't particularly frighten me. I had been in the hospital many times before, having had a very active and carefree childhood.

Taking after an uncle on my mother's side, I was born cross-eyed. After several surgeries during childhood, I am now left with good vision out of one eye. The other tends to wander about when I am very tired. There is a fancy name for this-- "amblyopia." Though I didn't know this term until I reached adulthood, I always will prefer it to the pejorative, "walleyed." Does anyone honestly think I am trying to focus on a wall, instead of on the subject at hand?! I wore glasses for years, my father trying to make it easier for me by using humor. He dubbed me "Four Eyes." The nickname stuck until, at 16, I was told that I no longer had to wear glasses.

This was my earliest experience of the miracles possible when patient and science join forces to recover that which has been lost.

Next, I had my 12-year-old molars extracted as they would not come loose, tenacious as their owner, I'm afraid. However, this time, the hospital stay was fun! My sister was in the bed next to mine having her wisdom teeth removed. Misery loves company!

When I was in the sixth grade, I went to a party where some of us decided to have a chicken fight. Somehow, while onboard my not-so-sturdy steed, I came loose from the saddle and toppled to the ground. I cushioned the blow as I fell, by jamming my hand onto the floor. Not so bad for the hand, but the wrist was a gonner.

Still further into childhood, when I was 12, I was out riding in the fields near the stable where I took lessons.

Unfortunately, the only instructions as to what to do if one beast ran off from the others, was to yank the reins with one hand, while holding on for dear life with the other. The horses were not listening well that day. Mine dashed away from the group, refusing to obey my hearty yanks, nor the increasingly anxious voices of the trainers beseeching him to return.

When I hit the ground, all I can remember was being yanked up into an ambulance and carted down the hill. The pain was excruciating and I remember not much else until, awakening in yet another hospital bed, I realized I had to pee. I watched my roommate haul herself up while the nurse settled the bedpan underneath her.

"Nothing to it," I thought. Grabbing the "trapeze" bar placed above the bed to assist in the endeavor, I pulled upwards.

"AAAAHHH!" I screeched. Needless to say, my broken leg was not quite ready to withstand that much pressure.

My friends signed a huge card and my family gave me a big teddy bear to keep me company while I was in the hospital. Outside the window, friends and family gathered once in a while to wave hello. They weren't allowed to visit for the first few weeks, but the view of them from the window (smiling to beat the band and waving ferociously) helped me make the best of it. It reminded me that my family was with me and my friends, not far away. It never occurred to me that I might not return to the same level of activity I had had before the injury.

Well, that is, with one exception. I never rode horses with such fearless abandon after that.

Later, at age 17, I was out for a bikeride near home.

As I crested the hill a 1/4 mile from our house, I saw a boy just ahead of me riding down the hill. As I approached rapidly, he must have heard me, but thought I was coming on the right, because he took a sharp turn to his left, right into me.

"Hey!!!" was all I could muster as I veered hard to my left. But, alas, it was too late. The boy escaped with a few scrapes and scratches. I, on the other hand, went head over handlebars. I landed ever so gracefully with a resounding "klunk," breaking and dislocating my shoulder.

"Hey, Carol!!" a friend yelled overhead, "Hang on!"

Hallsey, a good friend, luckily happened to be on the road in his car at the time of the accident and dialed 911. I heard the sirens as they approached, the boy sobbing over his mangled bike.

"Oohh! My friend's bike! He's gonna kill me!"

All healed without me being any the worse for wear. I felt comfortable albeit, once again, in bed at a hospital. Based on experience then, this was a place in which I felt confident and secure.

Sometime later, my mother took me to see a private doctor, just to be sure. He consoled her, "Not to worry, Holly. It won't leave much of a scar. No one will be able to notice it, "as if that was her main reason for concern.

As I grew older and (so I thought) wiser, I leaned more and more towards being more alert, thus avoiding further calamity!

CHAPTER 5
Home

It takes hands to build a house but only hearts can build a home.

Author Unknown

Home is where the heart is.

Pliny the Elder

The first few days home, I spent lying on the couch in the family room. Dozing on and off throughout the day, I continued to write, as I'd done in the hospital. Somehow, it was comforting for me to do so. Writing was one of the few things which seemed not to have changed and brought me the same pleasure it always had.

When Luis arrived home at the end of the day, we'd wrap each other in a warm embrace before he began to cook dinner. He always asked me how I was doing and how the day went.

More often than not I would answer, "Better every day, better every day." It was my stock answer, whether I really believed it or not. Little did he know that his return from work was the high point of my day.

One day, "How are you, sweetheart?" as he came through the door.

As we held each other close, I was aware that something had changed. I was less tired and much more conscious of his body against mine. Because he felt this also, he, too, became aroused. Gently, he laid me on the couch and began to stroke my hair and cheeks. His hands moved over my body, hesitant at first, then with increasing confidence, as I responded to his touch. Slowly, ever so slowly, and watching my face as he did so, he removed my clothing, one piece at a time.

Cupping his face in my hands, I kissed him hesitantly, then with increasing passion as he responded. Our bodies melted together and, for that moment, nothing else existed except the two of us.

When he came inside me, I knew, for the first time, that I truly was home.

CHAPTER 6
Humiliating Myself

It is not the pain and the wounds that are the worst.
The worst is the humiliation.

Pascal

Throughout my life, up until that fateful day, I took my intelligence for granted. I was taught early on not to act or feel better than others in any way. My parents impressed upon me that to do so would be boastful and disrespectful, would be ignoring others' intelligence and their gifts, perhaps of other kinds. I was careful not to brag about the good grades I earned in school, nor my athletic accomplishments. If I had done so, I risked disappointing my parents and, thus, myself. This perspective served me well as I moved through life. People seemed to respond favorably and I eventually discovered that I, too, had gifts other than intelligence.

Just as when a child, I relocated every few years after college, considering those years at college a distinct segment of my life. Treasuring the fond memories, I moved on.

After being injured, I got a call from two friends who had been in my class at Dartmouth. They were attending our Dartmouth reunion and asked why I had not come to be with them on this august occasion. I replied that I was too embarrassed to do so, only now realizing how very intelligent they all were, and I used to be.

I referred to myself as "stupid" in those early years. I tried to cover for things which revealed my diminished abilities. I was, in fact, my own worst enemy.

Depression and all that it portended, perched, like a snake, ready to strike. I was not as capable, in those early days, of fending off the fear which threatened to thrust me into the jaws of depression. Following closely on its heels was despair, and I couldn't risk that encounter. I clung to expressions of appreciation from my patients, and from other coworkers.

Fortunately, friends and most at work who knew me well, treated me with respect. Because of them, I knew that I was not only "the woman who had brain surgery." I was injured, not incompetent.

However, there were those times in certain settings, when I felt desperate and demoralized. I know now that I was hoping for some acknowledgment of my efforts and was more sensitive to the lack of it, than others might have been. I am ashamed to admit it now, that I went so far as to elect myself for awards given to those who did good work for the community. Certainly the work I did as a volunteer teacher and "friendly visitor" at Juvenile Hall, might warrant such appreciation.

"Have you done any volunteering beyond Juvenile Hall?" a good friend asked.

"Why?" I asked. But she would not say why she was asking, just smiled mischievously. I was pretty sure she was submitting my name and assumed that some were submitting their own names as well. So, the next year, I submitted my name to the committee. Having done so I was rejected as a contender. No wonder! I also elected two other people. I told them that I did this in the hope that they would not be embarrassed to be recognized publicly. I also wanted to demonstrate how many of us were impressed by their work, even if they were not chosen.

Shortly thereafter, I received a call from a member of the committee assigned to decide annually who would be selected as employees who volunteered on their own time.

"Carol, I just got your nominations for the awards. Can we talk?"

"Sure, Yo," I said, "What's up?"

"Well, I know that you want to nominate these people, but you already told them that you did."

"Yes, I wanted to make sure it was all right with them before I did it. Sometimes people are shy and don't feel comfortable being in the spotlight. They're modest about their efforts, especially these two, as you know."

"Well, "she paused. "That's not the way we usually do things. The prizes are awarded to people who don't know beforehand that they were elected."

"Oh," I said, "Sorry about that. I honestly didn't know."

"That's OK, I guess. Can you come on over to the office and talk some more this afternoon?" she asked.

I agreed and went to her office later that day.

She greeted me, a pained and confused expression on her face.

"Thanks for coming over Carol. I just wanted to talk about the nominations again. Apparently, you nominated yourself as well."

"Yes, "I admitted, a sinking feeling in my gut.

"Well, we don't usually have people nominate themselves. This is supposed to be an award which is unexpected," she reminded me.

Embarrassed now, I responded, "Good grief, Yo. What's wrong with me? Of course I should've known that...."

I certainly would have realized that before. Embarrassed then, I tried to make amends by explaining, "Yo, I honestly didn't know and assumed that others were nominating themselves too."

She just looked at me and shook her head.

By now, mortified, I said, "I am so incredibly embarrassed! I'm sorry to have caused all of this. Since you're one of those who knew me before what happened to me, you know I would never have done this before, nothing like this."

"It's OK, Carol. I understand," she tried to soothe me. But, I put my tail between my legs and slunk away.

"Stupid, stupid, stupid!" I admonished myself. How could I've been so clueless?! Idiot!"

I realize now, in retrospect, that these unconscious and eventually humiliating actions, were futile attempts to preserve what shreds of dignity I still possessed. Ironically, they served to do precisely the opposite.

CHAPTER 7
Master of Ceremonies

We acquire the strength we have overcome.

~Ralph Waldo Emerson

Arn and Nannette announced that they were having a party and invited Luis and I to join them. You never knew, with Arn, what "party" meant, until you got there. He was a wizard of sorts and the best father any girl or boy could hope to have.

When we arrived, there were many people we didn't know. Some were dressed in unusual costume. Given the history of Arn's hospitality, this was not surprising.

We shared a delicious potluck meal, then assembled in the living room at Arn's request.

A serious expression on his face, he announced, "Tonight's a special evening. We're going to pay tribute to those who overcame the odds, who won out in the end."

Shifting gears, he beamed as he scanned the gathered crowd. Those of us to be acknowledged, were startled by his words. The rest of the assembly turned towards us with curious and questioning expressions on their faces.

Though briefly embarrassed by the acknowledgment, we quickly melted into the good intentions and heartfelt respect.

No fingers were pointed, nor requests for speeches, just a simple raising of their glasses in a toast to celebrate our survival. These early recognitions were like salve to the yet tender wound.

Though my identity was becoming synonymous with being injured, to some it served as an opportunity to express support and encouragement.

CHAPTER 8

Kindliness

He who visits a sick person takes away one sixtieth of their illness.

> The Talmud (BaBa Metzia, 30b)

No one is useless in this world who lightens the burdens of another.

> Charles Dickens

As each day passed from then on, I felt stronger. I left the house once in a while to get a breath of fresh air in the back yard or front porch. I began taking short walks outdoors, always carrying my cellphone so Luis could reach me. As I began to feel more energy, I welcomed the visitors who started dropping by.

As my father's mother used to say, "I always know when you're feeling better, Freddie. You're bored, so start getting into things again!" Wise words and I was no exception to the rule.

Gradually, as my contacts increased and I moved into life in the real world again, I became aware of people treating me differently than before. They seemed confused or misguided sometimes.

I returned to church after a short while. My faith had buoyed me through hard times, all of my life. One Sunday, our minister, for some reason and for the first time ever, split us into groups spontaneously, to discuss gratitude. One man hurried across the room, joining the small group of us already gathered there.

"Oh! I want to sit with Carol!"

Obviously knowing what had happened to me, he sat down and began to stare directly at me. I was uncomfortable, sensing he was hoping for some words of wisdom from someone who he thought had the answers. I sat silent throughout the discussion, frustrated and shocked by his actions.

Another day, I received a call from a man whose son had died in a horrific accident.

"Carol, my name is Ed Brown. My son was a friend of your sister's. Maybe she told you he died?"

I hesitated, wary about where this might be headed. "No, not that I can recall."

"Well," he continued, "We never had the chance to tell him goodbye. We're not religious people, but I've been wondering about what happened to him after he died. I so desperately want him to know how much we loved him and still do. I can't let go of that thought."

He dissolved into tears.

Poor man, he needed so much to know that his son was at rest, that the love he and his wife shared for their son, was not lost to them.

"I am so sorry for your loss, Ed."

Once again, I hesitated. Then, "I can't possibly imagine how hard that must be for you and your wife."

"Well, I just thought, since your sister says they were sure you were going to die, were that close, whether you could feel what it was like. When you were so close and didn't go, could you feel the love around you, even so?"

Wow. I struggled to be honest. I didn't want to mislead him, to offer false hope. I knew that others have claimed to "see the light," then return to the living. I had no such memory. I could tell him only what I knew.

"Ed, rest assured that, when I was unconscious, I sensed those who loved me. Not all of them were there physically, but I know their thoughts soothed me. And, I was not afraid; I wasn't."

He accepted that, but I don't know whether it actually helped. Such interactions never ceased to exhaust me. Trying to take care of others in my personal life, just helping them as I had done without a second thought before, seemed more draining now, more enervating than I could bear at times. I was trying to recover and to make sense of this world, unable to offer the comfort others thought I could, needing comfort myself over those first weeks.

Others honestly wanted to make contact, to support and demonstrate that they cared.

I was very tired when I returned home, but seldom was able to sleep during the day. But, I persevered, taking frequent catnaps, as I wanted to make up for my restless nights.

One afternoon, I was dozing on the couch when the doorbell rang.

No one had called that day to ask if I would welcome visitors who wanted to see how I was doing and to cheer me up. I was tired and didn't want visitors, some of whom came, not to comfort me, but to quench their curiosity. I lay quietly, not responding, as I was tired and trying to sleep. I hoped whoever it was would think I was resting and leave me alone.

"Maybe she just can't get up, or she's napping," suggested someone I would normally have wanted to see.

"That's okay. My lunch break will be up in a bit, so maybe it's for the best anyway," her friend responded.

"She's probably not wanting a long visit right yet. We can try back another day."

These were two doctors, friends of mine, who meant well. I was grateful that they cared enough to visit and were wise to try another time. They knew about my medical status, respected my privacy, and returned to work. Most important to me was that they had taken the time away from an incredibly busy job and a much needed break for lunch, so as to try and accommodate me. This virtually guaranteed they would be staying late that night to finish. What more could I possibly ask?

CHAPTER 9
Against the Odds

This research shows that sleep plays a crucial role in emotional processing and opens up doors for therapeutic avenues.

Els van der Helm

I was cautiously riding away from a house full of people. I didn't know them, but they were readying for a conference of some sort – – lunch included. I couldn't find anything I liked to eat and the talk didn't interest me.

I found my bike, leaning against the wall in the far corner of the kitchen.

Outside, I mounted it and pedaled away, coasting for a time through town. Main Street was closed and cars were directed to alternate routes. I reached the "Road Closed" sign and paused to enjoy the sights. A marching band of youngsters, red-cheeked and grinning ear-to-ear, were strutting their musical talent to the applauding crowd of parents, siblings, friends and neighbors.

I shifted gears and was diverted into a section of town where eateries and pubs lined the streets, catering to the after-work crowd seeking a libation and perhaps a meal at one of the restaurants.

Suddenly, I saw my father, talking to others at the bar of a social gathering spot. Try as I might, I couldn't seem to get his attention.

Finally he turned to me, "Hey, Cacks! (another nickname) What's up?"

"Nothin' much, Dad."

But I pleaded silently with my eyes. I didn't know what I wanted, but was just intensely aware of how lonely I felt.

I lost him in the crowd, straddled my bike and looked around for him a while, then gave up trying to find him or anyone else. I was crestfallen and oh, so very alone.

The bike seemed to have a mind of its own as I moved out of the crowd and began riding down a hill, avoiding sidestreets. I didn't climb, but suddenly found myself at the top of Mt. Diablo and began rolling down.

I felt fine, in control, when, suddenly, I heard someone yelling from up the hill, "Carol! Hey, Carol!"

Turning my head back up the mountain I saw Mike, a bicycling friend of mine for years. We both loved hillclimbing and that was his forte. He was equally thrilled by the reward for the climb. Stretching his slender torso forward, he moved his hands lower onto the handlebars and positioned his body to create as little air resistance as possible, as he gloried in the rush of descending.

Faster and faster he came, though, strangely, never gaining on me. He leaned dangerously as he flew around the curves, now directly in the middle of the road.

"Mike! Slow down, slow down! Pull over! What're you doing?!" I yelled.

I could see a car back a ways, coming around a distant curve above him. But, he seemed not to hear me, not to be aware of anything but the descent.

I pulled over, shouting frantically, "Mike, stop! Stop!!"

Then, suddenly, there was no sign of him! He was gone--like soap bubbles blown through a wand and swallowed instantly into the air.

I pulled over and kept searching. Finally, I began climbing back up the grade, thinking the worst.

Suddenly, there he was, rolling toward me, a triumphant smile on his face!

I awoke with a start and sat bolt upright in bed.

"What does that mean?! "I wondered. "Geez, what was he doing up there?"

I got out of bed and wandered 'round the house, hoping I would calm down. Finally, unable to fall back to sleep, I pulled out my trusty dream journal and recorded the nightmare. Suddenly, a wave of relief swept over me, and I knew.

Mike had been in danger, though he didn't know it. He rode hard to the summit, then rewarded himself with the descent. He'd survived, unaware of the potential danger, and knowing he'd had what it took, despite the odds. Hmmmm....and that reminded me of who?!

I had more frightening dreams after that one, but never again, one as intense.

CHAPTER 10
Back to Work

You were sick, but now you're well again, there's work to do.

Kurt Vonnegut

The welcome back and congratulations were sometimes humorous, always thoughtful and sometimes both!

Soon after I returned home and was able to drive safely to visit friends, Eva called me and asked if I would have lunch with her and some others from the department of Psychiatry.

"We want to welcome you back!"

"Sure!" I responded enthusiastically.

It would be so nice to see some of my friends outside of the work environment. And, how nice of them to take me out to lunch! I assumed we would be meeting at the little deli located in the same building where the Psychiatry department was located. This was the place most people from the department grabbed a bite at the noon hour. I looked forward to the luncheon.

They decided, instead, to meet at the Hilton Hotel, just across the street from the department of Psychiatry, a rather more private venue for the gathering. Unfortunately, I gallumphed in a bit late, first checking in at the deli. Good grief, the guest of honor not there on time! Because of their nonchalance, I was not embarrassed and laughed sheepishly at my mistake.

Joining the small group of them at their table, I was surprised to see a fresh face or two, people I hadn't known before the injury. I couldn't help but notice their discomfort as they sat quietly, at first casting furtive glances every now and then in my direction. Once the others welcomed me back, they relaxed, and everyone launched into a discussion of job related issues and their personal lives. I felt comfortable joining them in conversation and preferred that kind of interaction, as opposed to being in the spotlight I so often dodged.

CHAPTER 11
Miracles

Instruction does much, but encouragement is everything.

Johann Wolfgang von Goethe

Too often we underestimate the power of a touch, a smile, a kind word, a listening ear, an honest compliment, or the smallest act of caring, all of which have the potential to turn a life around.

— Leo Buscaglia

As I gradually returned to the life I knew, I was increasingly critical of myself.

Though I had downplayed my intelligence before, I now referred to myself as "stupid." I spent a great deal of time and energy sidestepping situations which threatened to shine a light on my presumed inadequacies. I treasured my privacy because, if left alone, the only harsh critic would be me. These were the times I most needed some hope, when anger was no longer cutting it as a deterrent to fear. I clung to the oh-so-timely kind words of friends, as well as to the progress being made in the field of neuroscience. These combined to bolster my confidence so that I could see myself as capable, once again.

Not long after the second seizure, at home, my mother drove me down to San Rafael in order to see a specialist, an "epileptologist."

While waiting, she went down to the cafeteria to get a cup of coffee. She started chatting with someone who, she was surprised to learn, was one of the chief administrators over both Santa Rosa and San Rafael Kaisers.

Eventually, my mother explained the reason for her visit to Kaiser San Rafael.

"You must be talking about our miracle girl, Carol!" Judy exclaimed.

When I heard about their exchange from my mother, I felt grateful. I was, to Judy at least, a "miracle," but, also, I was Carol. Whether as a nurse professionally or at home with her ailing child, Judy was and is, a compassionate and exquisitely sensitive woman. She saw me as both injured and inspirational, because of what I'd survived and how well I'd fared. Such interactions buoyed me with hope that others saw me as more than just someone who had suffered a traumatic brain injury.

Still, beyond positive aspects of survival, there were lingering things annoying to me and to others.

"Carol, where is the avocado? "Luis asked.

"Darn, I did it again. I know, you told me three times to put it in the cabinet. So stupid!"

I had the same problem at work.

"Well, where is your timecard this time? Please send it immediately or it will be too late for this pay period, just wanted you to know," Yon kindly advised.

"I'm so sorry again. I'll do it right away. All of you are such paragons of patience and shouldn't have to deal with this."

"Carol, you really should stop being so hard on yourself," she comforted.

Hanging up the phone I thought, "Stupid, stupid, stupid, Carol!" But, this time, less harshly because she'd been so kind.

One day, I apologized to associates for any problems I might have caused them.

"Listen, I'm really sorry if I'm causing problems. I really don't want my behaviors to reflect badly on others. Do you have any suggestions of what I can do?"

This resulted in an awkward silence, and I sighed. Though I had good intentions, the message must have been delivered ineptly, at best.

Some rolled their eyes. Others seemed embarrassed and told me everything was just fine. But I knew that wasn't true and wished I'd never opened my mouth.

One compassionate soul took pity on me and later left me a message, "Did it ever occur to you that maybe one of us is the problem?"

"No. Frankly, the thought never occurred to me." I replied.

Here again, a few simple words treasured and saved, especially for those times when I most doubted myself.

And then there was my friend, Lola. Not too long after I returned, there was a knock on my office door.

"Come in," I said, and Lola walked in. She was one of those very rare individuals about whom I'd never heard an unkind word said, nor heard her say an unkind word about anyone else.

"Carol, I know about what happened while I was vacation in Hawaii. I'm so sorry I couldn't be here to help and to welcome you back right away."

Her work was difficult and not a job most would choose, because of this.

"Oh, please. I know you had a lot on your plate to take care of when you got back. I can't imagine anyone being able to cover for all that you do when you're gone."

"Anyway," she said, "I got you a little gift for you while I was there."

She handed me a small gold box. Opening it, I stepped back in surprise, "Lola, these are beautiful!"

Lying in the box was a string of pink pearls.

"I love them, but this is really too much!" I exclaimed.

"Nonsense! I wanted to do something, and I wasn't here. Please take them. It means as much to me as it does to you."

Supportive friends (especially those who show you the respect of accepting your help in return) are crucial to find. Their simple words can provide you with just the hope you need.

But, my admiration for healthcare and the power of friendship, extended beyond my HMO.

Occasionally, I visited my chiropractor (Dr. Alec Isabeau) for a "tune up." I had benefited from his ministrations for over a decade at that point. He was one of the finest musculoskeletal practitioners I knew.

I asked him if he was familiar with the Snowden study (see Introduction) or other research which might be relevant to my situation. He already knew about the famous study of nuns who lived to a ripe old age with significantly fewer signs of cognitive decline than were found in most people as they aged. He knew that exercise was the most important variable in determining whether or not we will maintain a higher level of cognitive functioning as we grow older.

Since biking was no longer advisable (at least not in the way I rode before) Alec and a good friend, Jim, encouraged me to start running again. Both Alec and his wife Lisa (a coach for a high school crosscountry team) were lifelong proponents of running for health.

Alec recommended that I run on dirt trails in the park, rather than on the road. Trail running requires conscious placement of each footstep, constant readjustment to the altering terrain. He added that improving balance might be another factor in maintaining cognitive function. He was the first clinician I knew to recommend this, and long before the many who have done so since.

Besides that, I discovered that the expected endorphin rush was magnitudes greater than after a road run. Running had always appealed to me in any case. I won a few marathons in college, but switched to other forms of exercise after graduating. Trailrunning was, shall we say, a "no brainer." By tailoring my runs to the Park near where I lived, I added practicing balance to the list of positive variables recommended to help keep the brain fit and recover.

Again, someone had offered me a helpful strategy.

He also turned me onto a book mentioned in the Introduction--Spark--(by John J. Ratey M.D.) as well as to the next book by this author (co-authored with John Manning)--Go Wild. These books emphasized the impact of exercise on cognitive functioning.

I needed these ideas and thoughtful acknowledgements to carry me through difficult incidents and interactions with those who did not understand. Whenever I felt discouraged or tormented, I would go for a run and inevitably feel better afterwards.

As time went on, the decrease in my proficiency level became more evident, never to anyone so much as to me. By now, you certainly must get it-- I was my own worst judge.

But, that was also around the time I began winning half marathons. I jumped at the chance to share my excitement. After one race, I grabbed my phone and immediately called our closest friends.

"You go, girl!" exclaimed Austin.

After they checked online for me, Margie and Laura sent an email, "Wow! You came in ahead of all but three of the men!"

Once again, acknowledgement of my accomplishments coupled with encouraging words just when I needed it!

CHAPTER 12
Empathy

The greatest gift of human beings is that we have the power of empathy.

Meryl Streep

It takes a ratio of four adults to one child to allow humans to go on. This is the real cost of our big brains. This is why we must cooperate, and why tools like empathy and language evolved to enable that cooperation. All else of human nature is derivative of this single human condition.

Go Wild, by John J. Ratey M.D. and John Manning

Many of those folks who were thoughtful and wise, used similar expressions of concern. Empathy is a potent tool as I found, effective for both patient and healer.

I went to church with my mother one Sunday. Afterward, I was approached by the minister, whom I had never met before. He looked at me sadly and shook his head.

"Congratulations on having survived such an ordeal!" he said, well within earshot of others waiting to speak with him.

"Good grief! Does absolutely everyone know?!" I thought.

However, in this case, I truly appreciated his efforts to provide my mother with the support she had needed during my hospital stay.

There were also various attempts to offer ideas about what I would feel and experience after the injury.

Sometimes well-meaning friends suggested that I read books written by people who had suffered a brain injury of some sort such as a stroke or a brain tumor. These friends, no doubt, read the books in an attempt to understand, so they could help me feel less alone in my condition. Unfortunately, just as with pitying, their good intentions did not always accomplish their goal. Instead, I felt that I was again being identified by a diagnosis, rather than by the unique experience and the recovery I pursued.

There was one book I found particularly unsettling. The author had had a stroke. One morning, she left home to go to work. A few minutes later, she could not remember if she had flossed her teeth, or if she had performed other simple ablutions.

I think I was just as upset about my own memory being worse, as I was by the assumption that I would fit into the same box of predictable behavior as any other person with some type of brain injury. But, because I knew her intentions were good, I learned to appreciate that this was her way of showing it.

Fortunately, there other personal and professional characteristics which defined me. It was a relief to find that I could function as a capable therapist, that I had retained the skills necessary to treat patients. I felt even more proficient when working with patients who were trying to manage an illness or injury. This was not surprising, if you consider I could feel for them and understand their pain. I empathized and knew what it was like to be working with a body that has changed. Through recommendations built on a foundation of experience, I tried to empower them to discover their own.

I told them, "Try to remember that the answers, the memories which evade you now, still lie within you, just waiting to be accessed. You must give it time and be easy on yourself. You can't deny what happened, nor its impact. If others demean you, be angry when reasonable, lest you become fearful and slip into despair. That is a dangerous place to be and not worthy of you."

When I tried to explore research regarding the brain, I was often discouraged as well. Research was helpful in establishing etiology and symptoms as well as in making others aware of potential pitfalls. These endeavors (at least to the untrained eye) certainly (and thankfully!) explored ways to improve the chance of delaying or preventing the onset of dementia. However, researchers were less helpful in offering coping strategies, in focusing on maintaining and recovering what was possible, and in tailoring this to the individual's needs, after a brain injury. One does not recover what is lost with dementia, not yet anyway. But, there is much to explore about what is possible following a traumatic brain injury.

Predicting and insisting that I exhibited what most other victims did, only served to foster a sense of powerlessness, of surrendering to what was expected, of despair. This did not bode well for helping someone and certainly was not an effective treatment modality, if treatment was, in fact, needed.

Twisting my actions to fit the diagnosis, resulted in much the same thing. It may have served a purpose to others, though they might react similarly to circumstances, should they experience the same.

I hoped that such presentations would also describe the variance in symptoms from one who was injured to another. Being stuck on one symptom could lead to pathologizing, even when the supposed "symptom," is a normal response to a situation (e.g., pride vs. narcissism; sorrow vs. emotional lability). Those who came to conclusions before consulting with a patient would be necessarily biased, twisting supposed symptoms to match the diagnosis. (i.e., the diagnosis would predict the symptoms, rather than the other way around). As a result of such actions, an injured victim's boat would be left flailing in the wind of defeat, unable to convince others to come about, thereby relinquishing all hope of ever filling the sails again.

Even the best of intentions can be diminished when empathy is absent.

Similar in one way (because of certain films and programs) was the bias of people who equated autism with Asperger's syndrome, for quite a while. Thankfully, the difference has become clearer to the general public. There is quite a bit of variance on the autism spectrum and how each individual adjusts.

Similarly, one person's expression of injury to the brain, despite some common symptoms, is never precisely the same as another's. The way my compatriots were portrayed often played right into the generalizations based on predictions. I witnessed others who succumbed to such expectations, and collapsed.

CHAPTER 13
Embarrassment

Embarrassment is "a feeling of being nervous or ashamed because of what people know or think about you."

--- MacMillan dictionary

My progress and self esteem at work were inhibited by hurdles set at a height which was, at times, difficult to surmount. These challenges were based on the same assumptions made regarding cognitive functioning. I needed to overcome these barriers in order to remain on course in the race toward improving brain function and accommodating to changes.

When I attended periodic staff education presentations, occasionally there would be topics such as traumatic brain injury and symptoms of those suffering afterwards. Advances in neuroscience and neuropsychological testing were also topics. As written in an online resource, Wikipedia, "tests are specifically designed tasks used to measure a psychological function known to be linked to a particular brain structure or pathway. Tests are used for research into brain function and in a clinical setting for the diagnosis of deficits." The focus on "deficits" implies that such things as coping, variance and individuality, again, were not the focus of attention. Such statements could be misleading to the public. I was embarrassed that some might be watching me for 'typical' and expected symptoms, or translate something I might do as a supposed "symptom," even though it was an expectable response to the situation. I was fortunate that, when I underwent neuropsychological testing, there was also attention given to improvement.

Some clinicians who knew of my history glanced my way repeatedly during talks, presumably curious about my impressions, or pitying me. I squirmed in response, especially when I wanted to correct the speaker about his or her presumption that symptoms noted post injury, applied to each and every one of us.

One day, I happened upon an acquaintance I hadn't seen since I'd come back to work.

Clearly surprised to see me, she leaped up out of chair, "(
great to see you back! We were all so worried about you."

"Thanks. And how have you been, Jody?" as I adeptly changed the
subject (or, so I thought).

No dice.

"Fine. Yeah, you know, when you fell off your bike, we were terrified.
We never thought someone who rode as much as you did, could fall
off her bike."

"What?! 'Fall off my bike?' Is that what you said?!"

This was like salt being poured on a wound which was barely closed.

She looked at me, startled, knowing she had crossed some line, but
having no clue as to how she'd erred. I knew she meant well, but I
just couldn't bear the thought that, in addition to being labeled as
injured, I must also be 'stupid,' enough to have 'fallen.' And, "we"
meant that she was not the only one who thought the tragedy was
of my own making, my own carelessness.

I felt like the runner who is tripped up by a competitor in the final
lap of the race, appearing to fall on her own, as the other woman
crosses the finish line in first place.

"Jody, I did not fall off my bike; someone hit me!"

"Oh, we all thought you just fell. I didn't mean anything by it."

Suddenly, I realized that I was accusing her, just as I had felt unjustly
accused. I wasn't listening carefully enough for the meaning behind
the words. After all, she meant well, and really did care.

"I know, Jody. I am sorry for taking offense. It's just that I spend a great deal of time belittling myself for being worthless compared to the way I was before. Being stupid enough to 'fall off' my bike was tough to hear. My husband inspected the site and is certain I was hit. Obviously, you were just telling me you care."

"Stupid, stupid, stupid!" my internal tormentor smote me as I walked away. How could I react as though she were calling me a fool?!"

CHAPTER 14
Regret

Sometimes remembering hurts too much.

Jess Rothenberg

I celebrated my 50th birthday the next year, with an open house BBQ, Luis manning the grill. It was so good to see everyone! I'd had several seizures since coming home, and some of these friends had taken turns driving me to and from work.

However, I had regrets about that particular celebration. Misinterpretation (as I did of Jody's comments) travelled both ways, causing twice the dilemma.

Among the first to arrive were Kevin and Laura. I had walked their dog, Angie, each morning, for years prior to the injury. Angie marked the beginning of the young couple's relationship when they were living in Wyoming. Soon, Angie became an endearing member of their growing family.

"Carol, sit down; we have something to tell you."

By the crushed looks on their faces, I knew something was terribly wrong.

"Angie died while you were gone," Kevin choked, "She was sick for a while, but, in the end, she didn't suffer much."

The tears welled up in their eyes, as they readied themselves for my commiserating.

I turned aside for a second, composing myself, then replied, "Oh, I'm so sorry, that must have been very hard on you," as though I were comforting someone I'd just met, about a lost loved one.

They just stared at me, a mixture of shock and bewilderment at what must have sounded like a rather canned response. Since I offered nothing more, they turned away.

How could I explain that I was acting callous in order to defend myself from yet another loss? I wasn't even aware of this myself, at that point.

I felt so badly about being so insensitive that, later that evening, I tried to talk again with Kevin. I knew that the most I could hope for, was a chance to apologize and explain.

"Kevin, I really feel so badly about Angie dying," I began.

He shuffled uncomfortably, looking over his shoulder as though searching for a way to escape.

I remained silent and gave him time to pull his thoughts together.

"Yea, Carol, you must miss her too," obviously offering me a chance to redeem myself.

I beat a hasty retreat, "Well, you must know that I was only walking her in the mornings, to help out your young family."

He stared at me, "Oh, well, I see," as he frowned and turned on his heel.

That wasn't pity I saw on his face; it was anger. I could see it took enormous effort on his part, not to tell me what he really thought of me.

"Well, gotta go now. Laura and the kids are waiting," as he civilly (though swiftly) dodged around me and made a beeline for his car. He had tolerated just about as much of me, as he could.

Now, it was my turn to shoulder some of the blame. I had, in their eyes, been deceiving them all those years, pretending that I cared.

"Wait!" I wanted to say, but it was no use. How could he possibly understand when I wasn't even sure that I did?!

There was no time to try and make another excuse. Sadly enough, I wasn't clear about how people expected me to react in those days. This was only the first of many times I tried to rationalize (both to others and to myself) such impulsive responses.

You might guess what came next, "You idiot! What's wrong with you?!" my relentless critic accused.

I wrote a poem about Angie (thinking it might help) following the second ripping out of their hearts. I was like a pyromaniac, returning to the scorched forest felled in the flames, only to ignite and burn again what was left. Writing the poem may have helped me, but, I suspected, only made it harder for them to process the loss. Though they continued to deal with me in a civil manner, I knew things other than the loss of their beloved dog, had changed.

Still, Kevin being Kevin, he was not inclined to hold a grudge. He had heard of my attempts to gradually work back into roadriding. An avid cyclist himself, he admired this and invited me to ride with him.

Though usually competitive by nature, Kevin took pity on me and kept my pace. He also rode just ahead of me, in order to stave off any difficulties which might arise. I appreciated his recognition of my need to be athletic and to return to some sense of normalcy as soon as possible.

Already riding ahead, he couldn't have noticed the difficulty I had clipping in and out of my pedals, nor the fear I felt roaring down a steep incline. The ascents had always been my favorite part of rides.

However, now I felt as though I had arthritis developing in my hands as I squeezed the brakes so tightly on the descents.

Rich, another friend and fellow cyclist, agreed to accompany me on what was to be my last roadride. This took place on my next birthday. The ride, as it turned out, was an unpredictable gift, as well as a disappointment to me.

"Hey Carol, ready to go?!" he hailed, as he parked his red truck in front of our house, his bike in the back and ready to ride.

We saddled up, clicked our cleats into the pedals, and took off.

It was a leisurely pace, but, unfortunately for me, there were many stop signs along the way. I hoped he wouldn't notice, but I sometimes had trouble clicking my foot out of the pedals. I stayed a distance behind him whenever a stop sign was impending, so that he would've moved on ahead by the time I got there.

After yet another fumble, he suggested, "I just remembered, I have to meet Brooke (his wife) by 4. How about if we turn back a little early?"

I actually thought he hadn't noticed.

Rich never truncated a ride, so I was surprised and said, "Uh, well, OK, if you want."

That was to be the last roadride I would have with him, or anyone else for that matter. Still and all, that ride remains one of my fondest and most memorable ones, even after so many years.

(P.S. I never told Luis. I'm sure, by now, you don't need me to tell you why).

CHAPTER 15
Sensations

"It is not the strongest or the most intelligent who will survive but those who can best manage change."

Leon C. Megginson

Remembering how to clip my cleats into the pedals was a relatively short lived change, but other changes were not.

First of all, I noticed that my hearing was much more acute. Though this would seem beneficial in some ways, at times it was not. What might be mildly annoying sounds to others, were simply intolerable for me.

"Luis, would you please turn the television down?" I asked for the umpteenth time.

We figured we were a good team, in the end. His vision was 20/20 and I'd worn specs since I was a toddler.

These sensitivities (though improvement would normally be welcomed as we age) became a source of frustration for me.

"There he goes again, "I fumed.

The noise was unbearably loud, but Luis was only mildly irritated.

"Now Carol, it's not so bad this time, "said Luis.

"What?! You don't think that's too loud?!"

"Yes, it's annoying, but not really so bad."

The neighbor up the hill was plaguing us mercilessly with the melodies he and his band were playing.

"Playing," is a far too generous a term for the plaintiff tones showered down on all of us night after night. No doubt, in his mind, he was gifting us with the songs. We had no say this, so I took matters into my own hands.

"I'll be right back, Luis!" I said, as I ran out the door.

I had always been the one to soothe Luis whenever he got so angry that he could just spit. After all, I was a social worker and a therapist. So, it took him a while before he registered what I was going to do.

It was not so much the music itself, but the fact that this man was so inconsiderate of his neighbors. That really piqued me. I could feel a migraine coming on, pushed aside the confusion and substituted the more acceptable emotion of anger.

I caught sight of Luis in the distance, running to catch up with me after it dawned on him what I had in mind. Realizing his intent to stop me, I dashed up the driveway to confront the errant musicians.

"Would you guys try and keep it down a bit?" No doubt intimidated, the ringleader simply glared.

Then, playing innocent, he asked, "What's the matter lady?"

I was surprised that he was my age, though I should've known because of the era in which the songs were written.

"It's a weeknight! Don't you care that some of us have to go to work in the morning?"

They paused briefly until he turned around and motioned them to begin where they'd left off.

"Really! I'm sure your neighbors are fed up with it too," I attempted to reason.

Apparently, no one else had complained. But, I stood my ground, oblivious to the uselessness of my endeavor.

"Lady, you need to see a shrink!"

I thought this was a tad ironic, given my metier. I decided it was time to change course.

"Why don't you have some consideration for the rest of us? I know my husband is sick of all this too. And he is not going to be happy with you, or me, about this! We all better hope that he doesn't head up here too."

It was only later that I realized this might be misinterpreted. Luis, despite his upbringing, had never raised a finger to anyone and has a fuse longer than Job himself.

Just then, my hero appeared on the scene. My anger flew out the window, submitting to fear.

Some of these guys were really big. It suddenly occurred to me that Luis, in my defense, could become really angry and they might reciprocate.

"Hey guys," he paused, giving them time to assess. "the music is good, but I sure would appreciate it if you would hold it down after dinnertime? I leave for work really early in the morning, you know, just to beat the traffic going down to the East Bay."

This went on back-and-forth for a while. Then, they turned down the volume and told us that, according to city policy, they had until 10 o'clock to play music on summer nights.

Obviously, Luis's approach was more effective than mine these days.

Talking on the way home, Luis reminded me that my hearing was more acute than before the injury happened. I had to admit this, though I initially I had not.

Another night, some weeks later, a neighbor's dog began barking in the afternoon and continued late into the evening. Finally I was fed up and headed off in the direction of the noise. Luis wasn't home for this one, so I was on my own.

I approached the house and knocked on the door.

A deep voice growled from within, "What do you want?"

"Your dog, it's been barking all day. Are you going to put it inside or what?"

No response.

I noticed that the light in the window to the right of the door, was on.

I stubbornly marched over to the window and asked again, "Are you going to do something or do I have to call the police?!"

I knew he must be intimidated this time, as there was no response and the window closed.

Dejected, I headed for home.

The barking stopped a few minutes later. I guessed some of the neighbors finally complained--possibly about the dog, though just as likely, because of my whining.

"Still, maybe, I've got him quaking in his boots," I tried to convince myself.

A week later, the barking started again. No answer, again, to my insistent knocks, though I noticed his red truck was not in the driveway.

Next night, the same.

This time, my husband was home. He insisted on coming with me to the house, having heard it all before. He was never as annoyed as I was by the noises in the neighborhood. And, once again, the neighbors weren't either.

I marched up the street cloaked in anger. The red truck wasn't there.

"This isn't good, Carol," Luis said, as he drew up beside me.

"You're right. Let's go home." I said. I felt the all too familiar rubber hammer slamming up that side of my head, the pain engulfing my temples. I was surrendering to the pain, in despair of ever getting a good night's sleep again.

Fortunately, the dog never barked again after that night. The police had visited this neighbor, telling us afterwards that he left the dog out when he went on fishing trips. They sent him a letter, telling him he must leave the dog inside or they would be visiting again and handling the dog themselves.

One less annoyance, even though we had to enlist help from other quarters. These incidents engendered a disabling assault of pain every time, so it is debatable which was worse, the thoughtless neighbors, or the migraines.

Months later, yet another dog was yipping, this time right across the fence in our backyard. By now, I was an experienced responder. But, once again, no one was home.

I did not push the issue, so fearful was I that Luis would get involved and that I would suffer the incapacitating pain again. I let the matter go for a while.

I still didn't understand why no one else was complaining.

I called the police (poor fellows) and asked, "What do we need to do to get someone out here? This guy's dog is out of control, barking all day and sometimes at night!"

"We need more than one neighbor to call if we're going to have animal control come out and take a look, "the policeman explained.

My younger sister, Sandy, had quelled barking by feeding our dog peanutbutter when we were young. The poor animal. Lucky simply could not, because of the shape of her mouth, readily dispense with the peanut butter. I remembered this and, so, tried to poke peanutbutter through the fence while the dog was out there. Nothing doing. This was not a dog to be so easily enticed. In fact, the yipping increased in volume.

Luis and I both feeling out of sorts, I waited until he was changing the timing belt on the car, then slipped around the corner to confront the offender.

The owner of the dog answered the door, saying that he was the son of the man who lived there.

"I only visit occasionally and I can't leave my dog alone. I'm sorry, I didn't know he was bothering people. And I didn't know how long he's been barking like that. I'm really sorry," he said.

Finally, with at least some acknowledgment, I told him, "Yeah, it's been going on for quite a while."

"Please let me explain, My mother was sick for a long time, then recently died. My sister and I have been visiting my father as often as we could and, then, we were getting together to arrange a memorial service."

And, that all-to-familiar litany began, "You idiot! Why didn't you at least ask him first, instead of just assuming?! Stupid, stupid, stupid!"

I apologized, now that I understood.

"That's alright, that's alright, you didn't know," he reassured me.

"Thanks," I said appreciatively, as I turned to leave.

"Wait, please wait," he begged," Look, it won't happen again. We were just gone the whole weekend to get together with the rest of the family and have the memorial service."

Now, desperately, I reassured him that the dog was no longer a problem. I dragged myself home, ashamed of my callous behavior.

This time, the rubber mallet was not the result of anger, but fear that I had made matters worse. I chastised myself mercilessly for having been so insensitive. Later that night, when Luis returned home, I explained to him how I had humiliated myself and added to the pain this poor family was already experiencing. Once again, I was my own worst enemy.

"Oh, Carol, c'mon!" Luis said, exasperated, "That guy's been living there since before we moved in, him and his dog!"

Okay, add humiliation to sorrow, "Stupid, stupid, stupid!"

Would it ever change? Anger is not always strong enough to fend off fear and remorse.

Still, the guy behind us, for some unknown reason, never let the dog out again.

CHAPTER 16

Passions

Running is my private time, my therapy, my religion.
Gail W. Kislevitz

I have to exercise in the morning before my brain figures out what I'm doing.

Marsha Doble

The only thing better than singing, is more singing.
Ella Fitzgerald

"I could feel my anger dissipating as the miles went by--you can't run and stay mad!"

Kathrine Switzer

We gotta get out while we're young,
'Cuz tramps like us, baby we were born to run.

Bruce Springsteen

Though I no longer went roadriding alone in desolate areas for hours at a time and was more easily annoyed by sounds, some things hadn't changed for me after being injured. I still used the same methods to relax and revitalize. When given the support I needed, I could recover or adapt to many changes as well.

Some form of stress exists for all of us, but mine now surfaced in areas not consistent with the past. Work issues were troubling at times, though memory problems extended beyond work. I learned to accommodate and adapt as best I could. But, solutions were more evasive, like fish gliding past me in a swiftly flowing stream as I failed, time and again, to hook one for dinner.

Gradually, I gained confidence in my ability to quiet these worries, to trust in those methods I'd used before being hurt and to rely on their efficacy.

I was told, from the very start, that there were many things I would no longer be able to do. At first I believed this without thinking, giving up before I even tried. I became resigned to certain things, but this rode closely on the heels of despair.

Gradually, I learned that predictions were not absolutes. Sometimes, it was simply a question of believing in myself. I did not have to accept others' versions of me, as long as I appreciated the fact that I was, although different in some ways, still worthwhile.

I tried to tell myself, "I'm my own complete package--good, bad or ugly, I'm all I've got!"

There were certain activities which had always served to heal and soothe me when I was troubled or wounded. Some were creative (writing and singing) while exercise (mentioned earlier) set the stage for living life fully. Running and singing were recovered after the injury and, as before, often occurred simultaneously. Writing was maintained as a creative endeavor, often helping me to process difficult situations. These were and are, my passions. Each of these relieved stress and was cathartic in practice, grounding me in the moment and wrapping me in a garment woven of gratitude. They bolstered my confidence, were effective defenses and excellent coping strategies.

Prior to being injured, I sang constantly, simply expressing gratitude for my life. Perhaps the worst change of all, then, was finding that I could no longer sing well. I had always been able to harmonize at the drop of a hat.

When I first opened my mouth to sing, I was shocked. I couldn't remember lyrics to songs I had sung for many years, some since I was a child. Worse, no matter that I could hear the discordant notes, my voice would simply not sing on tune. Despite my best efforts, I would repeat over and over again what I had already sung incorrectly. Nevertheless, I continued to try, so loathe was I to lose this precious ally.

I made an appointment to see my neurologist, Dr. John Cassidy, after returning to work and to discuss management of seizures. I knew the doctor quite well and had attended his wedding not too long before.

Once we'd dispensed with reviewing the labwork, I asked him how his singing was coming along. John, always a fan of opera, had taken up singing later in life. He sang to his fiancée at their wedding, a song they both loved--"The Way You Look Tonight." That was enough to draw tears from the crowd, not to mention his lovely bride.

He really was quite good and it took little encouragement for him to break into song, regardless of the venue. His patients loved this as it diverted their attention, however briefly, from their troubles.

As expected, he graced me with a sample right there in the appointment room.

Afterwards, he asked me how things were going, how I was adapting to life after surgery.

"Overall, can't complain John. I mean, the migraines are a drag and sometimes work is tough."

I decided to share with him my recent discovery. After all, he too loved to sing.

"John, I tried singing again, but no luck. I just can't get my voice to cooperate!"

John suggested I might want to contact his voice teacher. "She's been giving voice lessons for longer than you've been alive. She's taught generations of families and I think she might be able to help you."

The next day, I called her, "Hello, Mrs. Brockman. John Cassidy suggested I contact you regarding voice lessons."

"Well now, how is John anyway? I'm flattered that he sent you to me and that he thinks I could help. What exactly are you interested in pursuing with voice?"

I tried to explain, "I suffered a serious injury, followed by surgery. I used to be able to sing, but, now, it's nearly impossible."

Further discussion and she decided she might be able to assist me in learning to sing again. I believed that the answers to our troubles lay within each of us, only requiring the right kind of encouragement and guidance, to bloom. So, we agreed to meet at an appointed time the following week.

"In preparation, dear, please bring along a song which you are prepared to sing."

"But..." I started, then stopped.

How could I explain more clearly, so that she would understand? I was there, in fact, to resurrect that very source of pleasure and release. I could no more "prepare a song" than I could sing in the carefree manner I had previously employed, that true passion in my life. And, if it were no longer possible, what would I substitute in its place?

I didn't see her again, realizing that standard singing lessons would not help me to recover what I feared I had lost forever. Instead, I carried on, trying again and again. I noticed that there were several instances in which I could sing a line or two of the song. I tried to remember some lyrics, then waited for the tune to match the words. Because I began to recover what I'd thought was gone forever, I kept trying.

Luis and I went to Larry and Justine's home for dinner one night. Bless his heart, Larry acted toward me just the way he always had.

"Carol, come in. We'll just sing a bit before dinner."

I had always loved singing with him, whether out paddling canoes on the lakes and rivers, or at home. The songs we used to sing were chosen by him for the most part and matched the rhythmic dipping of our paddles into the water.

"Let's try John Barleycorn! You always love that!" Larry encouraged.

"But, Larry, I can't remember the words."

"No worries. We can put the song online and sing it that way."

I was embarrassed and didn't have the nerve to tell him that, not only could I not remember the words, I couldn't sing on tune.

"Sorry Larry, I know I used to sing, but it's just not that way anymore," and the tears began to flow.

He encouraged me, saying, "Oh, come on Carol, just give it a try."

Again and again I did so, but it was always the same. Normally, when these kind of situations arose, I quickly resorted to anger, once again to avoid fear and despair.

Fortunately for him, I couldn't get mad at Larry, one of those few who protected and watched over my Luis, while I was still in the hospital. Eventually, after several attempts, he stopped inviting me to sing.

I have always suspected that his wife, Justine, had words with him about it. Like Esther, Steve's wife, she understood my pain and protected me. I thought she might have told Larry what he could not discern on his own. It was hard to keep being certain that the answers lay within me, as did the notes, after so many failures.

So many other friends and my family, believed in me as well. My dear friend, Nancy, sent me a CD of my favorite old time hits, as well as some new ones. Another buddy, John (a gifted musician himself) created a CD of uplifting music and gifted me with it on my birthday. Once she'd heard of my aspirations to sing again, my sister, Lynn, arrived at my doorstep with a CD player and explained how to use it. All of these expressions of concern enhanced my recovery of melodies by allowing me to listen and sing while exercising.

Sometimes I sang while riding my elliptical outdoors in my backyard. After the noises from our bothersome neighbor up the hill, I decided to check with neighbors on both sides, to see if I was inadvertently annoying them.

"Suzie, can you hear me making noise when I take the elliptical outside?" I asked my neighbor..

Before she could answer, I leaped in and added, "I know how obnoxious that can be, you know, inconsiderate neighbors, so.....?"

"What? When do you do that? During the day when we're not home?"

Relieved, but not sure if she were only placating me, I continued, "Yeah, it's during the day, but I know I can't sing worth a hoot!"

This poor woman. She denied again that it bothered her, maybe just wanting to appease me and move on.

"Well, if it does bug you, please let me know. Thanks!"

I kept it to daylight hours, not late, and with the doors closed most often. (Hard to keep my voice down when I was so exhilarated!) The same kind consideration held true with my neighbors on the other side.

Fortunately, Becky and Ray, were just as forgiving. We faced a more serious event later on, as you'll see, and they rallied to support us then, too.

"We are so lucky to have such terrifically tolerant neighbors!" I told Luis.

Needless to say, he agreed. Still, I thought it best to keep it down some anyway. No sense in rocking the boat!

I had discovered the magic mixture of exercise and song, enhancing a pleasurable endorphin rush (there are worse addictions) of a magnitude greater than either practiced alone. Together, they enhanced relaxation and regeneration.

Still, I longed to discover something to replace roadriding in my cache of outdoor resources. That was when running became such an important factor in my life. Fortunately, there was a compassionate soul, Jim, who recognized my longing for activity and suggested the viable substitute of running. He started me out on the trails, running with me but with him in the lead at first. This was just what my chiropractor had suggested I do. Jim slowed his pace and adjusted to times I was available (rather that the other way around) as he was retired. Best of all, we became friends over time and I will be forever indebted to him for giving me this gift (though, as you will soon see, I also had to learn the value of moderation!)

I had won several marathons in college, so hoped that running could afford me the chance to do something as well as before. If my brain could no longer be as reliable, maybe my body could be.

At least being in shape boosted my flagging morale, at those times when I was particularly low. Running distance afforded me some measure of pride. Only when running, was I completely content, entirely free from troubling thoughts. I focused on compassion and the importance of learning from experience, then educating others about what it has been like for me To Be Injured (TBI).

Most of the time, I ran in Anadel, a beautiful State Park near home. Meandering trails crisscrossed the hills. Rabbits, squirrels, turkey vultures, coyotes, and even the occasional mountain lion, roamed through the grasses and rock-littered fields – skirting trails beaten by countless pairs of running shoes, hiking boots and mountainbike tires, over the years.

During winter months, the majestic redwoods shouldering Richardson Trail, shielded from rain or provided a lush canopy to filter the sun's rays as they dappled the needle carpeted ground.

During the rainy season, rushing streams coursed into Lake Isanjo, where wild animals quenched their thirst after dark. Animals of another sort, straddled inner tubes above the dam and slipped into tiny inlets to skinny-dip during the day.

This was the place I most loved to run, less populated as I climbed up to the ridge, traversing the meadows.

One day I was running on the trails, reveling in and amongst the magnificent redwoods--a privileged visitor to Nature's cathedral.

Coming up the last rise in Richardson Trail, about 8 miles into the run, I suddenly opened my mouth and began to sing joyfully. I was so shocked, then euphoric, that I almost began to cry.

Instead, I kept singing, inciting smiles from those coming up the hill. As I rounded the last curve before the final descent, I whipped out my cellphone and called my mother. Somehow, I knew she would understand.

"Holly!" I said when my mother picked up the phone," Oh, listen! I can sing!!"

And, I proceeded to serenade her with an old Carole King song from her Tapestry album, followed by Wake Up Maggie. I remembered these lyrics for some reason.

Virtually every time I chose a group of songs, I sang my favorite, Amazing Grace. I was thoroughly convinced I could sing again, once I could harmonize to this one!

Did I mention that my parents have always been my biggest fans? Regardless of what I created or did, they were always in my corner, cheering me on towards attaining a life filled with joy, self respect and gratitude, again and again. When I was struggling, they stood by me. When I floundered in the face of defeat, they were always encouraging. Then, I could catch the smallest glimmer of hope, that faint glow, and hold it for just long enough to catch sight of my true reflection, buried, but still living, within me.

True to form, Holly exclaimed, "Oh honey! I can hear you singing! That's fantastic!" As always, her enthusiasm was infectious and any shock left to inhibit me, melted away instantly.

My running buddy, Jim, encouraged me too. He refrained from dousing what certainly must have seemed an odd passion at times, to someone also a runner. He actually encouraged my serenading, asking only I not insist that others to join in! And so, once again, support carried me forward, hopeful and not so afraid of failing, even though I did so repeatedly. Because of friends and family, I won back much of what I loved most, not the least of which, was faith in myself!

It took years to begin harmonizing again and to sing on tune the first time I tried a song. Sometimes, I put lyrics on my phone and carried it around with me on the long walks I took every week and at lunchtime. I went to places where no one could hear me, or when out canoeing on the lake, oblivious to and not caring about, those who snickered from the shoreline.

Occasionally, someone would wave and say that I had a beautiful voice or sing along. When this happened, I thanked them profusely, and was on a high all week!

As my friend, Al (a doctor, as well as a talented songwriter and musician) told me one day, "The best you can do is try, over and over again."

That, and never, never give up.

CHAPTER 17
Oblivious and Toasted

"There is nothing to fear but fear itself."

Franklin Delano Roosevelt

"Live and learn."

(Anonymous)

"When you resist something, it just goes to the basement and lifts weights."

Dana

I recovered singing, but exercise remained my primary form of stress management. This was just fine, at the beginning. However, in time, I abused this generous gift, not being aware that I was doing so.

I was less sensitive to bodily signals after being injured. Before, like others in fairly good shape, I took little time to recover from physical exertion and felt the need to do so less often than others.

But, after the injury, my awareness of thirst, hunger and fatigue were less perceptible than before. I had never sweat as much as others, and often did not feel thirsty enough to drink until well past the time it was wise to do so. But, after the injury, I was even less conscious of thirst. The same was true for being tired or hungry.

This posed serious threats to my health at times, especially when running served as an escape from disappointment. These thoughts inhibited me elsewhere, but any lack of validation or respect (from me or anyone else) couldn't touch me while I ran. When I won races, I felt a surge of pride I had not felt at all in the months before I began to run.

Not recognizing the impact at first, I drove myself to a dangerous degree which twice landed me in the emergency room.

The first time, I simply needed to be rehydrated. Later, with two liters of water intravenously aboard, I felt fine, a lesson learned the hard way. As you might imagine, hydration was a constant consideration in planning my runs from then on.

The second time, lacking antennae for fatigue as much as I should, I learned another necessity--to stop long before I felt tired.

I rolled out of bed one morning as the familiar encroaching pain marched up the right side of my head. The rain was sprinkling down from dark stormclouds looming above. I was getting used to the pain and the signals that sometimes let me know when a headache was approaching. I thought about what Dr. Peterson had told Luis. I would have these headaches for the rest of my life. So, I tried to accommodate. If I caught it early enough, I could take an Imitrex and, generally, at least take it down a notch. After swallowing the medication, it helped to move around some until it took effect. (Maybe it got into my bloodstream more quickly?). Another woman at work had migraines too, and commiserated. Sometimes it's true, misery does love company. Stress seems less when it's shared.

It was my day off, so I put on my running shoes and ran a mile or two on the street to Anadel State Park.

"Migraines!" I said to convince myself, "I can outrun them!" I was so tired of them interfering with the life I was trying so hard to recreate.

But, it didn't last. Unfortunately, I'd just made another mistake at work.

"Carol, your member satisfaction scores have dropped. They were always stellar before. Let's talk about it." The goal of improving them was always added to my annual review.

I was pissed at myself and how this might affect others, so I decided to use an instrument entitled "minMPS" and presented it to every patient for their feedback. This provided me with quick response, rather that the "random choice" of patients for the larger Member Patient Satisfaction (MPS) survey used throughout the facility. Though nothing more was asked about it, I found it worthwhile to take what patients offered as criticism, in any event, so it was worth doing. I did this for at least five years.

Scores rose some, but never enough. I was frustrated that I didn't satisfy every patient as I had before. I found myself constantly saying I was sorry, sometimes before I knew what was wrong.

Finally, I remembered a line from a play I'd seen years ago, "I'm so sorry! I didn't mean to apologize!"

From then on, I resisted the strong temptation to apologize for everything. After a while, I realized that I was apologizing for just being me. Eventually, with this in mind, I decided to refrain from saying I was sorry for everything that went wrong. I learned to pause before opening my mouth, to consider if I was at fault. Then, if I were not to blame, I refrained. And, I advised patients to do the same.

"After all, when we apologize, who is automatically at fault?" I asked, "That's right, you are!"

When stress increased, I turned to running more and more.

I asked myself, "Why should I stop if I'm not tired?"

This lack of feeling tired proved to have embarrassing consequences on one occasion. That was a day now inextricably rooted in my memory, a lesson learned after running in a distractingly beautiful place.

I was so frustrated and disgusted with myself, after a particularly humiliating day, that I ran over 20 miles in the state park later in the week. I did this by linking all of the trails into one run.

As I was running home, I saw my compassionate and forgiving friend from my days as dog walker, Kevin, working on his bike in his garage.

He was usually interested in anything athletic.

"Kevin, I just ran 22 miles up in the Park! Wow! That's great. Now I know I can run a marathon again, like I did when I was in college!"

Kevin was an avid athlete, roadriding being his sport of choice. He once gathered some friends together and they rode to train and raced together, even in France. His enthusiasm was infectious.

I composed a little tribute to him after a particularly prestigious competition, in honor of his achievement and ability to motivate others. I was relieved that this poem (unlike the one about his beloved dog) was less offensive.

The same could be said about the day I stopped to see him.

"That's great, Carol, congratulations!"

One week, I ran very long runs twice, proving to myself that I was holding fast to my success. I valued running, just as other supportive friends recognized and encouraged. However, they didn't know how excessively I ran.

All I cared about was that I didn't feel ashamed of myself for a while. The headache after that run with the migraine was severe, as you can imagine.

The next day at work, I began to feel a bit dizzy. I was worried, so called Luis and told him. I didn't want him to get another phone call like that terrifying one, some years before.

"Hi honey, it's me. I wanted to let you know that I'm a little dizzy and that there's nothing to worry about."

He was silent for a moment, then said, "Carol, hang up the phone. I'm going to call Steve now on his cell." (Steve was one of two doctors who had rushed to the hospital and translated medical language for Luis).

Minutes later, Steve came into my office, "Carol, Luis just called me. Let's get you into an appointment room and take a look."

I did as I was told, though hesitated because I didn't want the medical assistants to know what happened and how foolish I felt. One medical assistant I knew well, sensed my hesitation anyway and calmed me down.

"Who's roomin' you?" he asked.

When I answered, he quickly soothed me with, "Jason? Don't worry, then. Jason, he's the Man!"

A few minutes later, Steve joined me, "Carol what have you been doing this week?" I told him about running up in Anadel.

"How far?"

"I'm not sure exactly, but at least 20. I tried to cover every trail in one run."

He sent me down to the lab, wanted to confirm what he, no doubt, already knew.

When I returned, he said, "Carol, your electrolytes are in the basement. Go and drink water and relax. Eat something as soon as possible, maybe take an electrolyte pill or drink one dissolved in water."

I did is I was told, and continued with the electrolyte replenishment throughout the next two days.

I told him I felt better, though, once again of course, I had a splitting headache.

Soon after, for some unknown reason, I got dizzy again. I was confused because I hadn't been overdoing it, hadn't been running excessively, and had plenty of fluids on board. So, I knew it wasn't electrolytes or dehydration. Luis took me to the Emergency Room, where a young doctor walked us through the "rule out's."

I was in tears and Luis's face was constricted with fear.

The nurse who called us into the appointment room, patiently took my vitals.

"Not to worry. It's not that bad, really," said the sympathetic doctor.

His brown eyes sparkled as he explained what he thought was a fairly simple reason for the problem. What a relief! There was nothing wrong with my head (relatively speaking) and my bloodwork and blood pressure were fine, i.e., no stroke or seizure.

He explained that it might be due to 'calcium deposits', floating around in my ears, as far as I could understand. He didn't know how long it would last.

Luis loosened up, then collapsed into a chair.

"It's called vertigo and we don't always know what causes it," the doctor told me. "It can come and go unpredictably. They take a while to dissolve, but then you feel fine again." He shrugged and I beamed at Luis.

"If you keep feeling nauseous, try some Meclazine."

So, off we went pick up some Dramamine at the pharmacy.

"Phew!" Luis muttered.

I took his hand to sturdy myself – "Thanks babe, what would I do without you?"

Later, I called and spoke with an advise nurse, who, as it turned out, had the same problem. She said that this "idiopathic vertigo" could come and go throughout the rest of my life unpredictably. I found some exercises online, which helped to reduce the discomfort. Fortunately, the dizziness was only slight, not disrupting my functioning much except to cause some nausea. I took a day off when it initially happened, until symptoms dissipated.

"Never a dull moment, eh?!" I joked with my parents and closest friends. My primary care doctor, Dr. David Pastran, was informed about my trip to the emergency room and I was scheduled for a follow up appointment with him. By now, I counted him as a friend. I sent him a note through email, about the experience:

David,

The advice nurse scheduled an appointment,
Which really might be a waste.
If it's just the same old, same old,
Feel free to cancel posthaste!

If so, be so kind as to drop a line,
How long is this vertigo likely to last?
Appearing drunk while walking around,
Is really a pain in the ass!

Getting up from prone position,
Always sets me reeling.

Lying down is great, but standing,
Yuck, that awkward feeling.

Frankly, I'm not really too concerned,
Only yet another malady.
Having considering everything, I've decided,
Someone else's turn it must be!

But, how could I have thought it was anything serious, after all my experiences?! I had thrown my poor Luis back into the nightmares of that other time when he was so helpless, like a tree once flattened by the wind, stretching back upright, only to be leveled once again.

I was also afraid that others who were not so supportive, would discover my limitations. The migraines were worse, as expected, when I felt helpless and afraid, when running and other passions for life were not enough to save me from despair.

I learned, over time, to accommodate to these changes. More water, more stops to refill, more singing---all in my favor as I tried to manage my disappointment in myself and the anger and fear so typical of trying to get back 'on track' (trail).

The positive aspects of running had blinded me to what was necessary. I was so allied to the advantages, it took longer than it should have, for me to grow aware and to make changes. Thankfully, I learned from these incidents. Whenever I plowed through an ordeal and learned something from it, I was increasingly more confident that I could resurrect my innate patience and amiability, while growing stronger through the process. This established an enduring sense of capability, of setting a goal and accomplishing it. I had recovered something from my past and had nourished it to remain.

CHAPTER 18
Half Dome

One's best is sufficient.

Irish proverb

An affirmation of my ability to better regulate my physical activities (and still enjoy myself) came when a group of us from work (hardy souls) ventured out to climb Half Dome in Yosemite National Park. This opportunity to show myself what I was still cable of doing, was afforded to me by a dear friend, Rorie, who was helping to organize the trip.

It was 90+ degree weather that drought--plagued year. We climbed all morning, as it grew hotter and hotter. I was in pretty good shape at the time, set my own pace and reached the base of Half Dome ahead of the others.

I stared at a set of cables stretching up the face of the rock and watched as the first few climbers pulled themselves, hand over hand, up the cables, step-by-step on the small wooden planks attached at intervals along the way.

"Hey Sam! It's okay! There's a whole pile of gloves!" yelped one very excited young man.

Knowing that others may not have brought the necessary gloves for climbing, some considerate climbers had left their own at the bottom of the cables for anyone to use.

After waiting a bit for my compatriots to appear, I decided to go ahead up the cables to the final destination with unknown companions. I knew I might never have the guts to do it if I waited any longer, so I walked over to the bottom of the cables.

After reaching the top, I was greeted by a panoramic vista of National Forests, majestic mountains and clear lakes below, so breathtaking and well worth the effort!

Walking around the top of Half Dome, others began to join me. I noticed the cables getting more crowded and the going, slower. Most were young adults, though there were some middle-aged folks like most of us and a few children.

As I started to descend, one man encouraged his 12-year-old, "Come on honey, you can do this. I know you can!"

Unfortunately, the little girl was not so sure. It was all she could do not to cry, her lips trembling, and near tears. I'm not sure whose ego was being boosted, but the dad looked very proud of her at the top. Given her broad smile underneath a few tears, I can only guess that she was daddy's girl.

Later, waiting at the bottom of the cables for my husband, I started talking with a young woman who was busily taking notes and counting as the climbers went up.

When I asked what she was doing, she explained that she was participating in a research project and living fulltime in Yosemite Valley. She was being paid to count the number of climbers each day, so hiked to the top many times a week.

She told a small group of us about the history of Yosemite, but also expressed some reservations. She was frustrated by the fact that her calculations could not be exact. Some people, every so often, hiked up and climbed the cables before she could reach the base in the morning. It was actually not permissible to climb at that hour. She was unable to count these folks, so was annoyed at this glitch in her research project.

I missed the photograph taken of the other climbers and the Physician-in-Chief of our medical center, at the top, as I was already hiking down the mountain with others--my loss.

One of the physicians joined us as we descended and stopped to marvel at Vernal Falls.

He sidled over to me, a friendly smile on his face, "Carol, how about if I take your picture, there, with the waterfall in the background?"

Delighted, I beamed into the camera, both thumbs up! Some months later, the photo appeared through email at work.

"Carol, I was just looking through my photo albums and discovered this. I thought you might like a copy."

Well, I certainly did want another photo to add to others from that memorable trip.

I teased him, "Thanks! Having taken a look, I encourage you to give up your day job! Your hobby is obviously yet another of your many talents!"

The evening after the hike, we gathered at the little restaurant attached to the motel where we were staying. We shared a meal large enough to satisfy our significant appetites. Light conversation and laughter permeated the room, the air conditioning much appreciated as we lounged in overstuffed chairs before the meal.

That is, until someone noticed that I was eating with chopsticks. I caught the questioning look and felt uncomfortable. I had been eating with chopsticks for 35 years.

By the time I finished graduate school, I was practicing a "macrobiotic" diet. Living in Berkeley at the time, no one batted an eye. I often went to the Macrobiotic Center to eat and to file away recipes. This very nourishing food regimen was developed years before in Japan and spread to other parts of the world. A friend of mine had used this diet to bolster men suffering from AIDS early in the epidemic. It not only nourished their tender bodies, but gave them some hope in their battle against this ravaging disease.

The diet was highly nutritious, and included no meat, lots of brown rice, no processed or fast or artificially sweetened foods, plenty of vegetables and sea vegetables. This is similar to the nutritious diet now recommended to most patients by their doctors.

I learned, from this diet, about the benefits of eating very slowly, savoring each bite, and using chopsticks to encourage this change in habit. The food is more thoroughly digested before reaching the gut, where further digestion takes place, more nutrients in the food being absorbed. The jaw is arguably the strongest muscle in the body per weight, so chewing slowly and more than usual, helped relax the jaw and part of my neck.

Children were interested in the chopsticks, so I always carried an extra pair for them to try.

This time, however, my eyes met those of the patron eyeing me with a disparaging look. I was confused. It hadn't occurred to me that my use of chopsticks could be cause for derision. After using them for so many years and never having to explain beyond the simplest statements, to those who asked.

The patron then motioned to his wife sitting next to him and rolled his eyes at me. The food slipped from my chopsticks and I dispensed with any further attempt to eat.

"Stupid, stupid, stupid!" the critic in me chastised.

When would I learn to be more careful? Though rarely, the chopsticks could be misinterpreted as a desire to be centerstage. Surely there were times in other venues when this would be a laughing matter, but I was too embarrassed to consider it humorous.

After we came home, Steve Rich, our dear friend and the Chief of Family Medicine, was interviewed about the trip for an internal Kaiser publication. He mentioned therein, that I was the first one of our bunch, to reach to the top of Half Dome. (He was one of the few people who might fully have understood the significance of this small accolade). That may not have meant much to others, but my heart swelled with pride.

Unfortunately, I mentioned to some friends about climbing ahead of others. They congratulated me, but word got around. Like anyone else, when I was proud of something and acknowledged for it, I assumed others might be enthusiastic. I even crowed a bit, I am ashamed to say. Given the lessons of childhood, this was verboten.

Some were displeased with the recognition, though I never knew why. I assumed they were not aware of how difficult it was to clear the medical and physical hurdles erected by the injury. Being acknowledged meant the world to me, if only to challenge the "stupid" label I had adopted for myself.

Still, my friends congratulated me, as I did them, when they "summited" their own personal mountains.

Later, a thought occurred to me. I had been desperately seeking some form of recognition for what I'd achieved, aware of my limits and the need to drink lots of water. Since I was physically strong, the climb was not so much of an effort. I know now, that I was mistakenly clinging to all that I had left of myself--my physical capabilities, singing and, my lifeline--writing.

CHAPTER 19
Self Respect

Self-respect is the cornerstone of all virtue.

John Herschel

A friend's eye is a good mirror.

Irish proverb

It was not always enough to recognize accomplishments on my own, I'd learned. Rewards I sought from others often came at a cost which was very trying at times. Denial came in handy then, but was not enough to overcome encroaching despair, were I not encouraged, once again, by good friends.

A friend I knew from college was visiting one day. Luis and I had been planning to visit him on the day I was injured. I told my friend how disappointed in myself I was at times.

"What do you mean? "he asked.

"It's hard to explain, just a feeling."

He went on to discuss one of the reasons he had wanted to get in touch with me. He wanted my professional opinion about something. Actually, the issue was right up my alley, so to speak. I offered him what I could and he said it was good to have my perspective.

Puzzling about it later, I asked, "What made you so sure I could help?"

"Carol, honestly, you seem the same as you were before. Can't really see any difference."

And Sandy, my youngest sister, "Carol, would you talk with Trev'?" Trevor was her older son, readying to leave the nest and set out in his own.

"Sure, what about?"

"Well, you know he wants to go to a really good school and all, and, being 'Mom,' I wouldn't have as much influence, if I gave him advice. That's right up your alley. Could you talk with him about this?"

"Sure, love to!" as I hugged her. She couldn't possibly have known how good it felt to know she still considered me to be "smart" enough to advise him and worthy enough to be of some use to her brilliant son, Trevor.

Finally, this one from my oldest sister, Laura, after I sent her a small amount of much needed funds at Christmas. (I'd learned long before this, over many years, that if I sent a personal check, she'd refuse and rip it up, thinking I couldn't afford it. So, I resorted to money orders and she had to comply).

"Cacks, thanks so much for the money!! I took all the kids to their favorite restaurant, and had enough left over to go up to the L.L. Bean outlet with them." (I knew that taking them out, seeing them enjoy themselves, was the best gift she could have).

Yes, I was her sister, not someone who couldn't survive or have something to offer. Nor was I just feeling sorry for her, raising her five kids. I was me, simply expressing my affection and concern, as she did for me.

I swung like a pendulum, back-and-forth, between hope and reality. But, as always, I gravitated toward those who, like my friends and family, recognized that I was Carol, someone who still had a brain.

CHAPTER 20
Dinner with Friends

Feeling this way was a particular kind of horror, having the emotions without the memories.

Cassandra Clare

Two of our dearest friends, then and now, were Steve Rich and his wife, Esther. As I explained previously, Steve was one of the few precious people who looked after my Luis when I was in the hospital. It was Larry and Steve who stood by his side every time he spoke with the surgeon about my progress or lack thereof. He made sure that Luis got some rest and went home occasionally.

Once we returned home, friends invited us to dinner at their houses for homecooked meals. Sometimes I had to leave early because of fatigue. When Steve and Esther invited us over, we readily accepted. They planned to ask another couple, knowing I would appreciate preparing how to react to others when they asked about the injury. I could practice this in a safe place before I returned to work.

Besides, it would be good to get out of the house and not feel the need to pretend when I was too exhausted to stay any longer. They understood completely and, without having to be told.

When we got to the house, their dog, Lily, announced our arrival by barking and gallivanting about until we came in. Once convinced that we were not intruders, she discarded her protective stance and switched to nudging for a good scratch. She kept me distracted, so I wasn't aware of the other guests in the room.

"Carol! Luis! Good to see you both," Steve welcomed us.

He turned to introduce us to the couple who had arrived before us.

"Tony, this is Luis and Carol."

"Wow! You look fantastic! And after all you've been through!" he said. Fortunately, Tony had heard about the injury, as had so many by that time. I didn't have to explain the basics.

"Oh, and this is your wife?" I asked.

"Yes, this is Shelly."

Shelly was a delightful woman with laughter infectious enough to complement her husband's endless repository of good humor. Any discomfort I might have felt, quickly evaporated.

After the meal, Steve turned to me and asked, "Carol, are you comfortable telling us what you remember from that day?"

"What exactly do you want to know?" I asked.

Suddenly, I felt a wave of relief. Tony and Shelley were people I didn't know personally. Maybe, through just talking about it, I could process some feelings. Since he and Steve were both Chiefs of Medicine, I didn't have to try and explain any of the still intimidating medical details. It also occurred to me that, through telling the story, I'd be proving to myself, as well as them, that my long term memory was not impaired.

I began at the start of that fateful day.

"I drove with Luis to work early in the morning, dropped him off at the refinery, then went to a staging point in Martinez. Priorities to the fore, I slipped behind a bush for a quick pitstop."

Here, I paused for a moment in relating the tale, chuckling to myself, as I recalled the impetus for taking care of business before starting a trip. Luis and I were traveling to Florida (a lengthy trip) when a young flight attendant insisted I return to my seat due to mild turbulence. I regretted that, at her age, she could not fully grasp the urgency of the situation. I tried to explain that, for an older woman, the distance between, "I have to go," and, "I really have to go!" is quite short.

Since then, I have had a new and adult perspective about my mother's sage advice to her four daughters prior to every lengthy car trip.

"Have you gone to the bathroom? You know we won't be stopping for a long time, so you'd better go now."

Returning to the day I was hurt, I continued, "Luis and I were planning to fly down to Los Angeles with our friend in his plane, later that evening. (Yes, you read it right, "his plane" and belonging to, quite possibly, the most modest person I have ever met!). We were going to visit Luis's brother as well.

I chose the longest route I could take for the ride. No one can enter the refinery without specific clearance, and I didn't want to wait too long before he finished working.

"You remember starting out?" Tony asked. "That's surprising. But, let's go with any details you can recall."

"Yup," I agreed. I took off up from Martinez."

The day was glorious, crisp and clear-- typical of early fall in the East Bay. Tawny fields of parched grasses waved listlessly in a gentle breeze, the last vestiges of summer before the winter rains greened the hills once again. As I crested the first hill and, before descending into the town of Crockett, I burst into song. There is nothing more exhilarating than climbing a steep, long upgrade, then speeding down the other side. Singing has always been a terrific way to express the feeling, so I'm sure there were many songs to follow.

By then, several glasses of water on board, I excused myself to use the bathroom, as memories of another day surfaced. I could never ride this route without thinking about another day when I had driven my car through Crockett to investigate damage inflicted on someone else.

During graduate school at Berkeley Schools of Social Welfare and Public Health, I spent some months as an intern for Child Protective Services. I visited homes in the area for signs of child physical and sexual abuse. My preceptor, Ann, was a pillar of strength and one of the primary reasons I was interested in completing my social work internship in Child Protective Services.

I remembered one particular day during that internship.

After climbing three flights of stairs in a grimy looking building, I knocked at the door of apartment number 36.

After several tries, I heard a meek voice from the other side of the door, "Who is it?"

"Mrs. Sanchez, it's me, Carol Gieg. I called you the other day about visiting."

"Please go away. I can't see you now."

I was familiar with this response, mostly from women who were afraid that their husband or boyfriend would find out that they had talked to a CPS worker.

"Mrs. Sanchez, I just want to talk with you for a bit." I knew better than to be too insistent.

Finally, after more cajoling, she acquiesced and opened the door just a crack (the deadbolt still attached) and said, "I know I said you could come over, but I really can't let you in just now."

Disappointed, I looked down at several bags of garbage, diapers, and who knew what else, sitting beside the door.

"Mrs. Sanchez, what are these garbage bags doing here? I can take them down to the dumpster, if you like."

That did it. She closed the door, slid the deadbolt, and let me in.

"You can come in now, but just for a bit."

I knew that meant the unspoken, "before he gets back."

She was about seven months pregnant, with a toddler tugging at her pant legs.

Hoping to help her relax, I opened with," So, Mrs. Sanchez, how are you and Joey doing these days?"

"Oh, good, jist good Mz' Gieg. Can't complain."

She stooped to wipe some peanut butter and jelly off his chin, then noticed it on his pants leg as well.

"Oh Joey! Sometimes I don't know what to do with you."

I glanced at the bruise marks on her upper arm as she reached out to him.

"How did you get those bruises, Mrs. Sanchez? It looks like they must hurt a lot."

Her bottom lip quivered. She took a deep breath, "Oh, it's nothing, really. It looks worse than it is. He was just trying to help me up after I tripped."

I returned to the original topic, not wanting to spook her, "I see, well, what about those bags of garbage? How long have those bags been out there?"

"Just a while. He really doesn't like me to go out of the apartment, Mz' Gieg; you know that. He's always thinking I'm trying to see someone else. I never am, though. I really don't want anybody else but him. I just wish he'd believe me, instead of getting so mad all the time."

Sensing an opportunity, I quickly asked, "You mean, he's the one who did this to you?"

"Yes, like I told you, but he didn't mean to. He was just trying to help."

Once again, she glanced out the window onto the streets. An enormous billboard, advertising the town's primary source of income, loomed over Main Street.

Domino Sugar was virtually the only big industry in town. The residents of the town depended on it for their livelihoods. I couldn't help but be struck by the irony of Mrs. Sanchez feeling so dependent on her controlling husband, their marriage devoid of the 'sweetness' portrayed on billboards throughout town.

"How long's it been since you were outside?" I asked.

"Oh, well, I really haven't felt like going out much, except when I go to work at night."

Mrs. Sanchez was a waitress on the evening shift at a local diner.

"Where is your husband, Mrs. Sanchez?"

"He just went out for a bit, a short bit, Ms. Gieg. Be back any minute."

I knew this was her way of telling me that I'd better leave soon.

"Okay. Let me just take a look at Joey."

"Joey, come and talk to the nice lady."

I quickly introduced myself to the little boy, "Hi there, Joey! You sure must like peanut butter and jelly, huh?" I teased him.

While he held his comic book, she stood by as I glanced over the parts of his body which were exposed. I playfully and gently patted his back and rump. He giggled, no sign of pain or fear. And, fortunately, no bruises. Her husband had limited his abuse to Mrs. Sanchez--this time.

"OK, it's really time for you to go now, but thanks for coming over."

"I'll go. But if you want any help sometime, for you or Joey, here's the number for CPS and the police." Just as she did, I had my own not-so-subtle way of telling her that I knew the bruises hurt her more than she would admit and that they weren't the result of him trying to "help" her after she tripped over the garbage.

I knew I would be reporting to Child Protective Services (CPS) and reviewing the day with my supervisor, Ann as, clearly, Joey was at risk. CPS was mandated to try and reunite families, if possible, but only if the child's safety could be assured. I hoped Mrs. Sanchez would accept the help when it was offered.

She wrapped one arm around her little boy, held him to her side and, without a word, she took my card and slipped it into her bra. Driving through town, I caught a glimpse of his truck, sitting in the parking lot of a local bar. He wasn't working; he was drinking. It was 4 o'clock in the afternoon.

Refreshed, I left thoughts of that day behind as I returned to the memory of that fateful day. Since Tony had requested details, I told them my likely choice of a few songs as I rode through Crockett (though without the story which brought the first to mind). No surprise, it was--Rosie Strike Back, by Roseanne Cash:

"Rosie strike back, Rosie strike back.
Hit the road and never look back.
You can't suffer your whole life living like that.
Get goin', don't pack,
Take the baby and the clothes on your back,
Keep walkin' Rosie,
Strike back."

Then, James Taylor:

"When you're down and troubled, and you need a helping hand,
And nothing, whoa, nothing is going right,
Close your eyes and think of me and soon I will be there,
To brighten up even your darkest nights.
You just call out my name, and you know wherever I am,
I'll come running to see you again.
Winter, spring, summer or fall, all you got to do is call and I'll be there, yeah, yeah,

You've got a friend."

I hoped Mrs. Sanchez had someone like that in her life.

I left that memory of her inflicted pain and injury (so reminiscent of my own) and continued where I'd left off.

"After passing by some refineries, I rode into Pinole Valley, where I stopped at a fire station for a drink of water and to refill my water bottle from the hose outside the building.

"Wait!" interrupted Tony, "you remember that much!?"

"Of course."

"What's so surprising?" I thought.

"I pedaled on, past one of the entrances to Briones Park, then continued to the bottom of the last rise before returning to Martinez. That grade is indelibly stamped in my mind as I'd ridden it several times before-- Pig Farm Hill."

That was it, end of story; I drew a blank at that point.

"I don't remember anything after that, until I woke up in the hospital."

Suddenly, I felt nauseated. I excused myself and headed straight for the bathroom again.

I took a few deep breaths and splashed some water on my face. Once I'd recovered somewhat, I returned to the dinner party. Apparently, Esther had had a word with the two men while I was gone. I could tell, because the conversation was kept strictly away from the previous topic.

CHAPTER 21
Writing

If you don't want anyone to know anything about you, don't write anything.

Pete Townsend

The only way you can write is by the light of the bridges burning behind.

Richard Peck

Writing is it's own reward.

Henry Miller

Just as running and singing were treasures, so was writing. Before being injured, I could express myself fairly well using the written word to communicate my thoughts. I had always found it cathartic to write, so it only made sense that I would return to it afterwards.

Shortly after waking from the coma and consistently after that, writing helped me adjust to my new life and to focus on what hadn't changed, rather than on what I'd lost. I could turn to it for the assurance that something undeniably 'me' was still alive, despite loss of hope and trust for a time.

Some who cared, after reading what I had written, recognized my efforts as being helpful to me--that I was not denying the truth. Unfortunately, a few with whom I shared my story simply ignored it. Because this writing was meant eventually to support and share with others in pain, that hurt.

As I've mentioned, I used anger to bolster denial of their assertions. Some who were not medically trained in such an injury (and some who were) did not recognize the possibility of variance in outcome or misinterpreted my actions.

My HMO referred me to post-surgery service providers in my community, some of whom did not account for how my condition might be different from others with similar diagnoses, nor if I might have changed from my initial status.

One such referral was to a speech therapist. Having never had speech therapy before, I expected nothing in particular. Perhaps I should've taken the hint when the darn place was so hard to find. I was given the address, but not directed as to exactly where the office was located within a large cluster of professional offices.

I eventually succeeded in locating the office marked with his name. Opening the door, I stepped into an empty waitingroom consisting of a few chairs and no receptionist. Confused, (but unwilling to leave after the significant effort I'd made to find him) I sat down and waited.

Eventually the door to the inner office (sanctum) opened and a patient emerged. She looked dejected and forlorn. Shortly afterwards, the door opened again to reveal an enormous mahogany desk behind which sat an officious looking man.

He crooked his finger at me without rising, "Good morning my dear. Come right on in and take a seat."

As I approached, he waved his hand towards the chair in front of the desk and returned to charting his note on the previous patient. After a few minutes, he set the notes aside. Picking up a new sheaf of papers, he slapped them down onto the desk with some vigor.

"Well honey, I guess you've been through some tough stuff. I have reviewed your case and have begun to make some plans for you, regarding your speech and speech therapy."

I didn't respond, but what was there to say? He wasn't asking for my input or comment, so I just sat and waited.

Then, "Well, dear, before we begin, let's agree to a few things." His voice slowed to a drawl.

"It is likely that you will be confused about what we do here at first. Don't blame yourself as this will work against what we are trying to do. If, while I am explaining, you are confused or need to ask a question, just raise your hand and I will stop to give you time to collect your thoughts and express yourself as best you can."

I was frustrated that he would speak to me in such a condescending fashion, but agreed and he began. The questions were very elementary and I did my best not to smile. He leaned across the desk towards me, as I sat in a chair which was so small that he peered down at me from his lofty perch.

After about an hour, he said, "Well, we seem to be out of time for today, so we'll schedule another appointment for you to come back. Don't you worry, my dear, I will write down the date and time for you. You will forget it if I don't. By the end of my evaluation, I will have a plan made especially for you and you'll feel better."

This time I asked, "What exactly do you mean by 'plan'?"

"Oh, my dear, don't you worry about that. I have a lot of experience in the type of injury you sustained. All you need to do is trust me and we will, I promise you, make progress."

Since I knew that even to survive such a severe injury (never mind remain fully functional) was exceedingly rare, I felt even less inclined to return.

As I hurried toward the door, anxious to leave, he said, "Oh, by the way. We will want to get some idea about how well you can do on your own. All I ask you to do (and I know it will be difficult for you) is to write sentences on a paper and bring it back to me when you come in again. Try not to get too frustrated with yourself as this will only make matters worse. Remember, you and I are going to work together and, I promise you, we will see progress."

Needless to say, I was not impressed by the fact that he was going to make a plan without any feedback from me. I left feeling humiliated more than anything else, mixed with a good dose of anger at his assumptions.

But, I assumed he knew what he was doing, so I returned the following week. There was no one in the waitingroom, and I was on time for this visit. Again, I settled in to wait. Sometime later he opened the door, then returned to his throne behind the intimidating desk.

Again, he crooked his finger at me, "Come on dear, you can sit here," as though I would've forgotten where to sit. I was happy to be there, in fact. I had dispensed with writing the sentences, bringing, instead, a sample of the writing I had done since being injured. I was sure that he would be impressed to see how successful I could be and how much beyond his expectations.

"Now, honey, did you remember to do the assignment I wrote down for you?"

"Yes I did." I said, handing him the sentences, "And here's something I wrote after I was injured. I passed the papers to him. It was the story of what I remembered about the ride that day.

He read through the first few pages, and scanned the rest. When he finished, he laid the story down on his desk, shook his head and turned to me.

"Now, honey, you can tell me who really wrote this."

"I did," I responded, surprised by his assumption that I had not.

"Oh, sure you did dear," as he reached across the desk and patted my hand. "But, really dear, we're not going to make much progress if you are not honest with me."

That did it. I stood right up and headed for the door, his whiny voice beseeching me to return and calm down.

Now, I know patience is not a virtue of which I am abundantly endowed in all circumstances, but, frankly, I think I demonstrated considerable reserve in this case. I left the writing on his desk as testament to my proficiency.

I hurried into the waitingroom which was now filled with stroke victims and their loved ones. The hopefulness expressed in their questioning faces, gave me pause. I fervently hoped that his demoralizing attitude would not triumph over their hopes and remaining talents, once they engaged in treatment.

Afterwards, I considered what had happened. He had nearly made me afraid that my writing was no longer what it had been. But that fear was short lived. Anger, once again, had come to my rescue and defeated the fear. I knew writing was helpful in managing both the physical and emotional pain suffusing my body and spirit.

Some time later, a colleague won a contest in a local newspaper. He had written an original piece, not in his native language, but in Spanish--quite a feat. The author was very modest, and many were told of his accomplishment by a friend of his.

This inspired me. Since I had always found writing to be an effective way to express myself, I figured I would take a stab at writing something about the migraines which I would then (and always) have.

I didn't want the piece to sound like nothing but whining and complaining and hoped that whatever I wrote might appeal to others. They might benefit from knowing that they were not alone in their pain, that others were trying to manage similar difficulties and could relate.

I began by reading a bit about migraines and those who had suffered from them.

I learned that many people who were successful and from all walks of life, had had migraines. According to the National Migraine Association's report, in migraine.org, some were artists. (Vincent van Gogh, George Seurat, Claude Monet). Writers included Virginia Woolf, Lewis Carroll and others. Leaders mentioned were Julius Caesar, Napoleon, Ulysses S Grant, Robert E. Lee, and Mary Todd Lincoln. Elvis Presley suffered migraines, as well as psychoanalyst Sigmund Freud and philosopher, Friedrich Nietzsche.

More current sufferers were also listed. Elizabeth Taylor, Carly Simon, Loretta Lynn, Whoopi Goldberg, Kareem Abdul--Jabar and Terrel Davis had migraines. Recognizing others' success in overcoming migraines enough to excel, I was that much closer to writing about my own experience and, hopefully, to processing it.

Finally, with encouragement from Cinzia Garvin (an expert in pain management at my HMO's Chronic Pain department) I completed a piece and submitted it to a national newsletter. I was overjoyed and proud when it was printed in the American Chronic Pain Association's "Chronicle", during Chronic Pain Month, September, 1911:

Some Nights Are Like That

It is three a.m. and I am wide awake.

A familiar nausea taunts me. I have assiduously ignored its warning for the last half hour or so, before I lay down to sleep. I am simply not going to allow it to win this time. I am stronger than that!

Dreams pock my slumber and mask the warning of advancing troops up the right side of my head. They attack as an enormous wave of pain, progressing rapidly upward from behind, as well as over, the occipital ridge. The wave gathers reinforcements— more nausea and tears.

Fortified, they march without pause, directly towards the gripping stronghold of Trapezius. The troops surround and press inward. Sweeping their guns skyward, they take aim and shoot. The shots ricochet throughout my head and lodge behind my eyes. Satisfied in their mission so far, they pause to reload.

Fully awake now, I am livid. I grab my temples and squeeze shut my tearful eyes. True to form, I refuse to retreat and, instead, dig in my heels. I shift my head from side to side, seeking respite long enough to plan my counterattack, and determined to defeat this evil force attacking my head.

I plan to fortify my own soldiers with those weapons best-suited to defend my precious tender soil from the marauders.

But it is no use. Sleep is no longer anywhere near a possibility.

Pain advances again until, finally, I order a retreat, surrender, and grab for my medication. My lads and lassies break out the litters and begin loading their wounded comrades, and carrying them to medical attention.

I am submerged again and again, leveled by shots of pain even as my own soldiers attempt to stitch and mend me. Opposing troops, as though to pour salt over the open wound of this overwhelming defeat, wave the flag of triumph emblazoned: "MIGRAINE."

I call in reinforcements, swallow yet another pill, sit up or stand, take a walk, try natural vinegar recipes, ice packs, caffeine, and surrender to nausea. Soon, all's been spent. Now I can rest while my troops hold MIGRAINE at bay.

But I know the pain army will be back, once I recover enough to fight again. As soon as I am caught unawares—too fatigued, too hormonal, too traumatized, too allergic, too emotionally stressed, or too something I don't even know about yet—then will the troops gather; then will the wave swell; then will the attacks recommence.

Some nights are like that.

It all makes sense to me now. Writing kept me afloat. Support from others and singing calmed the waters. Running provided reassurance that I had the physical stamina necessary to paddle safely ashore.

Again and again, whenever I felt discouraged or afraid, I turned to these passions, to reinvigorate self confidence, restore hope, and to affirm that what I had to offer was still worthwhile.

CHAPTER 22
Luis's Passion

The marks humans leave are too often scars.

Chuck Paluhniak

Cuisine is an act of love.

Alain Chapel

Cooking is way of giving and making yourself desirable

Anthony Bourdain

"When we no longer have good cooking in the world, we will have no literature, nor high and sharp intelligence, nor friendly gatherings, nor social harmony."

- Chef Marie-Antoine Carem

Cooking is an art, a noble science: Cooks are gentlemen.

Richard Burton

If you really want to make a friend, go to someone's house and eat with him...the people who give you their food, give you their heart.

Cesar Chavez

Lack of memory affected my relationship with Luis for a while after I returned, that is, until he recognized that I actually was listening when he told me something, but just couldn't remember afterwards. Fortunately for me, he possessed his own coping strategies to help weather the trauma he experienced when I was injured, or, now, when I was forgetful. His brother and he explained to me that he developed these coping strategies early in life, to cope with a horrific upbringing. They were battered as children, often every day, and for reasons they seldom could fathom, nor ask, of their alcoholic and abusive father. Should either boy attempt to ask, they would risk yet more abuse.

Fortunately, Luis is one of those very rare individuals who not only survive physically, but spiritually, the threats to his very being.

Luis learned to cook from his grandmother when he was a boy, and in secret, because his father did not approve of males cooking. The kitchen was a woman's domain. But Luis persevered, aided by his loving "abuella" (grandmother) when his father was not home.

Luis and his older brother called her "la gruñona" (the complainer) but she never kowtowed to anyone and confronted head on those with whom she was displeased. Loving her was natural and the boys teased her mercilessly, though always with kind intent.

The kitchen was a warm haven, safe and secure enough for Luis's creative talents to blossom in spite of being raised in a garden devoid of tending.

One morning, Luis was in the kitchen with his grandmother making his father's favorite dishes, including "huevos revueltos y arepas" (scrambled eggs and corn flour bread). His father lay in bed, recovering from a drinking binge the night before. The tantalizing aroma of the food wafted its way up the stairs from the kitchen.

"Francisca, me gusteria desayuno, por favor?" ("I would like breakfast, please?") his father called.

"Por supuesto. Sólo un momento, por favor!" (Sure, just a moment, please) she called back.

Luis, focusing on the food preparation, suddenly dropped the spatula at the sound of his father's voice. Frightened, he turned towards his grandmother, a deer caught in the headlights.

"Berto, no. No te preocupes¡" ("Don't worry!") (Berto was Luis's nickname.)

Quickly, she grabbed her apron and tied it around her waist.

Trembling, he washed his hands in the sink, placed the dish he'd prepared at the head of the table, and sat down to wait. Eventually, his father arrived, glanced at the two of them and took his seat. Napkin folded into his lap, he began to eat.

"Ay, Francisca, esta es exelente! Como siempre." ("Francisca, this is fabulous! As always.")

"Gracias," she replied, quickly grinning over her shoulder at her grandson.

Luis ducked his head, beaming with delight.

"He likes it, he likes what I cooked!" He could hardly contain himself.

Suddenly, his father seemed to notice Luis for the first time.

"¿Que está ahí de pis¿ ¿¡No tienes tareas que hacer¿¡" (What are you standing there for?! Don't you have chores to do?)

Every Friday evening, his father wrote a long list of chores for Luis and his brother to complete the next day. He paid them a nominal fee for cleaning the cars, cutting the grass, washing the dogs. This, in addition to the mountains of homework given the children of Venezuela to be done over the weekends. They were kept busy and often didn't have much time to see their friends. Yet, as with most boys, Luis longed for any sign of his father's approval. Young Luis cooked many a breakfast and feasted on the delight of his father before Sr. Colina learned the true identity of the chef. He did not chastise the child, merely allowed Luis to cook breakfast on the weekends. (That old adage, "the way to a man's heart is through his stomach" comes to mind). And, for Luis, from then on, cooking was truly an act of love.

Even now, cooking remains a passion, it's fire stoked by the pleasure he gleans from others when they enjoy his food. It is a creative outlet for him and springs from deep within, helping him in ways I never recognized until I understood that this, in fact, was his passion.

CHAPTER 23
Relationship

Trust is the glue of life. It's the most essential ingredient in effective communication. It's the principle that holds all relationships.

Stephen Covey

Despite the techniques we had at our disposal, and the support we gleaned from others, the torturous acuity of my hearing, as well as pain and stress, put a strain on our relationship. Also, Luis had his own road to hoe with an irascible buffoon at work. Just when each of us was longing for support, neither one of us was available to help.

Sometimes, Luis would lament, "I miss my Happy Carol," the one whose natural optimism and love had carried him through days when the smothering pillows of childhood memories threatened to suffocate him. I wanted so desperately to help, but I didn't know which way to turn.

Our ability to communicate deteriorated, at times to dangerous levels. Both of us desperately in denial, we used anger to combat the fear of losing each other. But, sometimes, the fear enveloped us, and we tumbled down its slippery slope into the ditch of despair.

One sunny day, we hopped into the car to run an errand.

"Luis, head toward the mall, but turn left after the highway," I told him.

As we approached the mall, I reminded him.

Nothing doing. He put his blinker on to turn right instead.

"What's the matter with you?! I said to go left."

"I know, but that's not right," he corrected me.

"Yes it is!" I told him, aggravated.

"Now come on Carol, calm down, calm down. You'll see when we get there." I was so angry at being doubted, that I burst into a tirade.

"You don't believe me! You think I'm too stupid to know the right way to go, but I do!" I railed at him.

As he continued in the same direction, I grew more incensed. Finally, furious, I grabbed the doorhandle, preparing to leap out as he slammed on the brakes.

"What are you doing Carol?! Don't do that."

I started to open the door, then, startled, I pulled back into the safe haven of my husband. I regained composure with more than a trace of regret.

"You know it'll never change. Even those rare times when I'm sure about something, no one believes me. I'll never escape the 'stupid' label."

By this time, he'd pulled over.

I said, "Look, honey, I'm just going out for a walk. I know it's not your fault, really. I just can't stand it anymore. Even you think it too," as I headed for the highway.

Bless his heart, he followed me slowly in the car. Pulling up alongside me, he pleaded, "Please, Carol. Please get back in the car, You're right, I know it. I'm sorry."

Finally, and only because I couldn't stand to hurt him any more than I already had, I returned to the car.

"I'm really sorry honey. I'm the one who should be. You are not stupid; I am!" he insisted.

But I knew he wasn't. I kept thinking, "Why do I keep torturing him like that?!"

Neither one of us recognized what had happened until later. We were discouraged when neither of us understood the other's actions. We used anger to shield ourselves and, when it no longer could contain us, we felt destitute and so very alone. There were times when each of us felt helpless and reaching out to each other for the comfort that wasn't there.

These arguments usually occurred on Friday night at the end of a long work week. They were becoming more frequent and intense over time, reflecting our anguish.

The arguing usually started with a casual remark, taken wrong, then exaggerated, as the blaming began.

I was checking my email when he arrived home from work.

"Babe, what are the plans for this weekend?" he innocently asked.

We had decided a few years before that we would keep a calendar of upcoming events so that each of us could keep track on our own.

"We just talked about it last night and you chose the date. Remember? Just take a look."

"Oh, c'mon! Just tell me! Good grief! It's already been a long day, now this."

"Look, all I said was 'take a look.' We started using the calendar so neither of us would be responsible to remember."

It really had been a long day at work for him, plus the hour and a half commute.

But I wouldn't let him get off that easy, "Why am I always the one who keeps track? They're your friends too!"

And it went on from there, back and forth, until we started yelling at each other.

"Just listen to yourself! You know I'm right, but you won't say it!"

"No! And it shouldn't matter who's right anyway! Doesn't our relationship mean more to you than that?!"

Suddenly, Luis noticed that the sliding doors were open.

"Carol, stop. Look!"

"Oh, good grief! No!" I whispered.

The neighbors on both sides had kids. This was not the impression we wanted to give them. Talk about being embarrassed!

We stared at each other, shocked by our behavior.

We separated, each more afraid of ourselves than we were of the other. We retreated into opposite ends of the house to cool down. There, we sequestered ourselves for hours, afraid and, oh so very alone. Still, better to be alone and afraid for a while, than to risk destroying our relationship forever. We'd argued before, though never as badly as those days. It was like losing a best friend over and over again.

We decided to give couples therapy a try. The office was perched on the third floor of a recently-renovated Victorian and housed several psychotherapy offices. The faded beige chairs and worn carpet of the waitingroom, accented the hopelessness we felt and did little to mollify the tension between us.

A middle-aged woman eventually entered the room.

"Carol and Luis?" she asked.

"Yes," I answered.

"Right this way," and she ushered us into the room.

Luis hung back, eyes lowered as he followed us.

Once inside, we sat awkwardly on the edge of the seats, Luis eyeing suspiciously, the big box of Kleenex next to his chair.

She began with introductions, then described her cancellation timeframe and penalty, the cost of the therapy and her insistence on both of us sticking with the therapy as long as she advised, at least a few weeks, even if we felt dissatisfied. Her technique required some time to take effect. She insisted that we sign a contract before we began. All of this took a big chunk out of the '50 minute hour' allotted for psychotherapy. Glancing at Luis, I noticed that he was gazing about the room, then focusing on the floor again. Clearly, he was uncomfortable, if not bored. I wished she would finish her orientation, or, at least save the rest of it for after the session.

Finally, "Well," she began, "why don't we begin with each of you describing why you are here and what you hope to accomplish."

That seemed reasonable enough, and I was glad that she was finally beginning the session.

We shared our backgrounds, then I said we were hoping she could help us improve our communication.

Unfortunately, she launched into the usual (and antiquated) technique used in couples work, "Carol, I will ask you a question and you answer. Luis, tell her what you think she's trying to say before you respond, so she can affirm that you understood her correctly."

Luis slunk further into the seat across from her, apparently wishing he could disappear into its cushions. Ignoring him, she began directing her comments to me.

I tried to explain that we used to communicate well about most things, always trying to understand the other's point of view. We were having trouble doing that anymore. Unfortunately, she didn't take this on.

I tried again, "What I think we want to know (after our recent blow up) is that the way we say things, makes a difference. If we could get that far, maybe we could again provide the love and comfort we know the other needs."

"OK now," as she turned to Luis, "tell her what you heard."

He just looked out the window. "I don't know," he delivered with a long sigh.

Things went on like that for what was left of the fifty excruciating minutes. Needless to say, we didn't go back.

Next, we went to a conference given by Gottman therapists. This group had been trained to provide couples therapy, specifically.

That's when I realized, with enormous relief, that we could recover what the injury had nearly taken away from us. All it took was recognizing patterns, practicing a different response to disagreeing, then committing to change the habitual pattern consistently and with love. Despair retreated and hope prevailed.

We began to face difficulties together, arguing less as we adjusted to changes and renewed our commitment to each other. He helped me navigate and accommodate, like the sighted leading the blind. He listened to me when I cried out in fear, questioning myself and desperate for the validation I'd lost. I, in turn, stopped blaming him for everything and resisting his attempts to make things right.

I accented our reconciliation most days, by leaving little poems of love, humor, or to practice speaking Spanish between us.

When our 20th anniversary arrived:

Oh, Luis, My sweet love,
So dear and precious to me.
I would give you the whole world,
But that's not how we want it to be.

We create our own place,
With chosen family so true,
Those who remain with both of us,
No matter what we go through.

Our 20th anniversary today,
Destined to find each other by fate.
The years may pass forever,
Still, each day we celebrate!"

CHAPTER 24
Frustration

Failure is feedback.

(Dana)

Gradually, over those first months home, I noticed things other than my ability to sing, sensitivity to bodily signals and auditory acuity had changed. As I explained, I initially thought I'd lost capabilities, but was able to recover some of these. I accommodated to changes and maintained many which it was predicted I would not. Yet, other shifts could lead to humiliation or fear.

Before being injured, my memory was more than reliable; it was exceptional. This made my life so much easier than afterwards. How very much I had taken for granted.

Now, the simplest of things were hard, if not impossible, to recall.

I was driving to an appointment one day, when I noticed that the gas tank was nearly empty.

"Oh crap!" I thought as I pulled into the gas station.

"Geez! You fool! Which side is the gas cap on? Why can't I remember these things?!" I growled in frustration.

Jumping out of the car, I located the errant gas cap, and laughed (lamely) along with the customer at the pump next to mine.

"New car, huh?"

"Uh...no, used, or 'pre-owned' as they say, but my last car had it on the other side," I tried to divert his attention from my ignorance, uncertain if it was actually true, but hoping I wasn't lying.

Next, on to pumping the gas.

I had to read the directions and, unfortunately, a zip code requirement had been installed during the time I was in the hospital. I had trouble following cues on the screen about how to pump the gas.

I glanced around, thinking, "I hope he's gone!"

Gratefully, he was. I returned to the task at hand.

Once again, no dice. As I cursed at the darn thing, another patron joked, "Hey, do you need a hand or something?"

"Oh no! The pump doesn't seem to work (no mention of why from me). I guess I'll just go inside and have them reset it."

"Oh, been there--yup. What a pain!"

"I'm having some trouble with pump number two. Can you reset it for me?" I asked the attendant inside.

By then, thankfully, I had figured it out, pumped the gas and left. As I pulled out onto the road, I reviewed how to do this, speaking aloud. I'd learned that doing so helped to implant the memory more securely.

"What a jerk I am, and how embarrassing. That guy knew, I just know he did!" I spluttered, chewing on that humiliating event for the rest of the day.

CHAPTER 25
Safeguards

Wisdom is the daughter of experience.

Leonardo da Vinci

Though forgetfulness was trying when in public, there were other incidents more fearsome to me. Two, in particular, involved threats of humiliation and were related to management of my health.

One Saturday morning, I went out for a run. When I arrived home some hours later, I couldn't remember whether I'd taken my pills. I looked for the box where I usually kept them, but it wasn't around.

"What should I do, what should I do?!" I asked myself. Had I already taken them or not?

I knew my husband would be home any minute. He had witnessed me having a seizure once at our house. I couldn't bear the thought of him going through that again.

I swallowed nearly a full dose, and hoped for the best. But, after Luis returned, I thought better of it. Maybe I truly had taken a full two doses within five hours of each other. I closeted myself in the bedroom, reached the on-call nurse at Kaiser and told her what I'd done.

"Nothing to worry about, dear. You didn't hurt yourself, but we will be sure not to do that again, now won't we?"

No, I guess "we" won't, I thought. She must have taken a look at my chart.

"I guess not," I answered.

"We really need to be more careful. Is there anyone there to help you in the future, so this sort of thing doesn't happen again?"

"Oh, yes," I reassured her, just wanting to end the call.

I was so relieved, that I was able to ignore the nurse's condescending use of "we". Well, almost. Being treated like a child always stuck in my craw. I felt as though I'd fallen into a patch of brambles, the thorns punishing me for being stupid enough to be there, in the first place.

Better to be the angry adult Carol, than the child, fearful and inept.

CHAPTER 26
Fear

Many fears are born of fatigue and loneliness.

(Ehrmann)

The only thing we have to fear is...fear itself.

Franklin Delano Roosevelt

Once, on my day off, I went in to work anyway, just to have my quarterly blood tests to measure the level of my seizure medication. Afterwards, I walked over to Peets coffee shop and waited for Luis to pick me up. This would normally be a great opportunity to enjoy the day. I waited and waited, but still no sign of him.

Suddenly, I remembered--the seizure pills.

I kept them in a box marked with the days of the week, separate from all other supplements I took to enhance brain function (See: <u>Memory Bible</u> by Gary Small, M.D. Director of the UCLA Center on Aging, 2002, chapter 7)

Like most educated people of my era, my supplement arsenal was well stocked. I took vitamin D and calcium for bones, a multivitamin for general health, along with vitamin C, zinc, and the occasional echinacea and goldenseal for flu.

Included also (and perhaps more significant to me) were those things purported to promote brain health. Omega 3's, certain B vitamin supplements, vitamin E, coconut oil and tumeric, topped the list.

I know this meant that I probably had the most expensive urine in the world, but, so be it. I had long since overcome any skepticism I might have had towards supplements and medications. Even if some had had only a psychological effect, it was worth taking them because it gave me the sense that I was not entirely powerless to predict my own destiny. Hope is hope and much more inspiring than the fear experienced by doing nothing to help yourself.

However, medically speaking, the seizure pills were most essential. I had left for work earlier than usual one morning. It was my day off and I had not eaten the night before. This was in preparation for having my periodic labwork done to assure adequate seizure medication was on board. I was hungry after the blood draw, so headed down to Peets coffee shop where Luis would pick me up. I'd been in a hurry that morning and suddenly realized that I'd forgotten to bring along my seizure medication. I'd planned to take it just after completing the blood draw.

"Oh no! What if I have a seizure right here, in front of all these people?!"

It wasn't the seizure itself which most frightened me; it was the risk of humiliation. I scanned the area feverishly, looking for any place I could hide.

"Good grief, anything but this!"

I could see myself falling backwards onto the ground, shaking uncontrollably and terrifying everyone. I would have no control and, who knows, might even soil myself! I had heard that this could happen.

Worse yet, what if someone at work heard or saw! I couldn't bear any questioning of my professional capabilities.

"There!" I spied some shrubs at the far side of the parking lot, up against the fence. I dashed over and dove behind the bushes. Safe for the moment, I relaxed just a bit. I peeked through the branches, just enough to keep an eye on the front door.

Fortunately, Luis arrived soon.

I slipped out from behind the bushes and dashed toward the car, "Luis! Over here!"

Startled, he looked in the direction of my voice, then threw open the passenger door.

"Honey, what is it?! Why were you over there?"

"Oh nothing," I told him, relieved, "I just didn't want to wait inside on this beautiful day."

"Sorry I'm late, hon', there was a lot of traffic because the high school just let out. Want to stop at Oliver's on the way home? I need a few things to cook for tonight."

I looked at him and answered quickly, "Not now, if you don't mind. Could you maybe take me home first and then go?"

"Sure, sure, no problem, "he quickly answered, detecting the tension in my voice. We made it home without further incident.

It was only then that I remembered. The pills were actually time-released, so it was unlikely anything would've happened.

Lying in bed that night, I thought over the events of the day.

I blasted myself with, "Stupid, stupid, stupid! How could you have forgotten?!"

Once again, live and learn. After that experience, I always kept an extra set of pills, both in my car and in my purse.

CHAPTER 27
Face Erase

It is impossible to live without failing at something, unless you live so cautiously that you might as well not have lived at all.

J.K. Rowling

Memory is the treasure of the mind.

Thomas Wilson

Short term memory problems were less socially humiliating than were other memory challenges.

Things got worse after the fourth seizure. Recognizing faces was sometimes difficult though not with people I knew well. Some people in the medical field assumed that I would not recognize them, based on what was medically expected.

"Hey Randy!" I said. We were in the causeway on the way in to work.

"Hi Carol! Welcome back!" He paused, then, "What?! You remember my face?!"

I didn't know at that time all of what was medically expected, so answered, "Of course I do, Randy! Whaddya mean?"

"Well, we just didn't expect that you would! Great!"

How embarrassing and surprising. His comments were meant to acknowledge my recovery and compliment my progress, just as were Jody's. However, I was overly sensitive. There it was again, the seemingly ubiquitous "TBI" label.

I gradually learned that I did remember some folks. They were ones I had known well and saw frequently before the injury. Randy was one of these.

Sometimes, however, it was very, very difficult to recognize those I'd seen only recently or sporadically over a long period of time. I developed little, "tricks," to help me remember or to remove myself from a situation before I was found out. I literally needed to see someone most days a week for months, before I could recognize their face.

Worse, and often even more humiliating, was when these things happened at work.

"Hey Carol! Welcome back," chirped a colleague just days after I returned. I couldn't recognize the face, though it was familiar.

I stared at her blankly, then plastered the ever available, no doubt convincing, smile on my face.

"Hi, how are you? Good, good," I answered my own question before she had a chance to answer it herself.

"Gotta go!" I threw in her direction as I ran past. Very busy, indeed, as I tried to avoid further discussion.

"You know, I don't think she knew who I was!" she reported to the director later.

I tried to be angry at both of them, but I was running low on the fuel which drove me forward. I threw it into neutral to conserve what little energy I had left, feigning surprise at their presumed assumptions about me.

But soon, I ran out of gas, and I stalled out in fear. What if others found out?!

"Stupid, stupid!" I cursed myself, "Just remember, for heaven's sake!!"

Before the injury, I not only attended, but organized everything from camping trips to picnics for my module of colleagues. Afterwards, I limited social gatherings to only those essential for being a part of the team. I was scared of how foolish I would look, were I not to recognize someone with whom I'd worked for so long. It was not consistent enough, if they were at the other end of the module or worked only occasionally at our end, for my brain to memorize the face.

Each year, our module in the Family Medicine clinic sponsored a holiday party. I was afraid to go because of this problem.

After a while, Luis and I had a system worked out between us. If we approached or were hailed by someone, I would say hello, then pause.

Luis would stick out his hand and shake, saying, "Hi! I'm Luis, Carol's wife, and you are?"

I would act embarrassed (often the truth!) that I hadn't introduced him. The colleague invariably and naively delivered that much needed information, and none the wiser. Or, so Luis and I hoped. There is always the chance that we, actually, were the naive ones.

Then chanted the masochistic refrain, "You idiot! Get it together!"

Often, the recipient of my blunder would kindly chuckle.

If they hadn't been there more than a few months, a medical assistant or doctor, looking shocked, might say, "What?! It's me, Carol!"

Alternatively, they might simply assume that I didn't care enough to remember.

This left me feeling so anxious and frustrated that I often made it worse by offering excuses or apologizing profusely the next day.

"Yeah, well, whatever," they'd say, disdainfully dismissing me.

"Hey John!" I hailed a friend as he was on the way to his office early one morning. I wondered why he was headed in the wrong direction.

Confused, he responded, "Carol? It's Al." I tried to cover my mistake by saying, "Oh, of course! Can you believe – you guys look so much alike!"

Again, I hurried past. Fortunately, I didn't have to worry about Al. He was a doctor, and also the friend who had urged me to keep trying to sing. He understood more than most, without me having to explain. As he hightailed it for his office, I was sure he was trying to save me from further embarrassment.

Unfortunately, he did not succeed.

Another day, I was looking for something in the local organic food grocery store.

"Do you happen to know where the bulk food is? You know, like granola, flakes, oatmeal, muesli? I'm shopping for breakfast," I grinned.

Sure, "he said, "it's just over there," he pointed, "second section on the right."

"Thanks," I said, turning down another aisle to pick up juice first. After wandering for a few minutes, I located the cereal, shoveled some into bags and returned to the front of the store.

As I entered the line at the register, I realized I had forgotten something. I returned to the aisles and looked for someone to ask where the toothpaste was located. There was a sales associate, (as they are called these days, just in case this is news to you) at the end of the aisle, stocking shelves.

"Excuse me, I just asked someone where the cereal was, but I forgot to ask him where I can find the toothpaste?"

He turned to face me, then looked puzzled. I literally had not recognized his face, though I was quite familiar by now, with that puzzled expression.

It was the same young man.

I hastened to chuckle, a practiced (and usually convincing) ploy to keep them guessing, I wanted him to be amused, rather than judgmental of my inadequacies. These little ploys were helpful to me in maintaining my self respect, the first step in drawing respect from others.

Another such incident occurred when I was at a house concert one night. A patient hailed me.

"Hey Carol, "he said, "come on over and meet my wife."

I told my patients before beginning our work together that, when in public, I would wait for them to acknowledge me first before I approached, just to maintain confidentiality. We were a smaller community then, so this was a distinct possibility.

He quite clearly was comfortable with me being there. He looked at my husband expectantly before starting the conversation. Fortunately, I recognized his face after many psychotherapy sessions.

Unfortunately, I could not remember his name to introduce him to my husband.

Just as so many times before, I managed to shake his hand and, after chatting about the concert briefly, I moved on. I didn't want to give him time to ask me anything further, nor ask me to introduce him.

When he later asked me in session why I disengaged so quickly, I said that I simply did not want him to feel uncomfortable, nor anyone else.

"I wasn't. That's why I reached out to you."

"Oh, sorry," I apologized and, nodding respectfully, accepting his view.

I was in Safeway a few weeks later, picking up a few things for Luis.

While there, another patient spied me.

He approached me, saying, "Hey Carol! How're ya' doin'?"

"Hi!" I responded, "How are you?" I had no clue who he was, having met only a few times. Nor, of course, could I remember his name. Fortunately, his voice clued me in and I remembered the treatment.

I always took copious notes so that I would remember, thus implanting the memory more, just by writing about him. Focusing on the sound of the voice also gave me a clue.

His wife rescued me without even knowing it, "You really saved our marriage. He thinks so highly of you. Me too! Thanks!"

"You're welcome." I smiled. "Sorry not to acknowledge you first. Remember, I told you I wouldn't?"

"Oh, right," he said.

I saw him in the store again another day, though on his own this time.

When he hailed me, I thought, "Geez, what is his name?" Try as I might, I simply could not remember it.

"Hi!" as I skirted past him, not stopping. As it turned out, this was not the best plan!

This time, he was not puzzled; he was miffed. But, what could I say that would allow me to appear accommodating while still maintaining credibility and objectivity in his eyes? I was at a loss and knew this would impact the therapy. I wouldn't be credible to him if he knew my history to the full extent. Likely, he would be watching to see if I understood, or would pity me, rather than focus on his own needs. Thus, therapy would not be effective.

Later, he asked why I acted that way.

"Well," I paused, at a loss for words, "it's better if you acknowledge me a second time on your own."

Talk about credibility problems now!

When I got home, I tacked a little Post-it note on the mirror on my side of the medicine cabinet, with, "Safeway embarrassing moment" and his first name, tacked beside it. I had learned much from experience over the years. The possibility that I would remember was much better if I attached something unique or unusual about that person to his name. If I pronounced that name out loud for a few days, all the better. Visual and auditory hints made on the spot, implanted memories and made them more accessible to me in the future.

After experiencing many of such interactions, I read about a method for remembering a person. (<u>Memory Bible</u> by Gary Small, 2002). If I practiced focusing on a particular characteristic (unusual haircut, a tattoo, a birthmark) chances were much better that I could recall. If I wrote down the characteristic with the name, or repeated aloud that characteristic several times, while thinking of him, that helped even more.

Making a habit of these tricks, through practice, increased my proficiency for using them.

Each week, after meeting with my faith community, I would jot down a particular characteristic or interaction with a fellow congregant, then leave it in the glove compartment, to be reviewed prior to the next service.

I practiced something similar when I met with the adolescents at Juvenile Hall. I was a volunteer, a "friendly visitor," meant to provide these youth with an adult who was objective and nonjudgmental, into the boy's life. I couldn't bear to be disingenuous with these young people who'd so often been recipients of same. They trusted me to be a confidant, someone who expected and encouraged them to be honest.

So, I told each boy upfront, that I took notes after each session about what he had told me, that I was getting older and forgot things more. Interestingly enough, these kids who had been much maligned and ignored during their lives, were impressed that I would find them interesting and important enough to take notes.

And they were right. I was gaining far more from the experience of being appreciated, than they ever were from me!

After all was said and done, again, sometimes things ended up in my favor.

CHAPTER 28
Concentrate

The true art of memory, is the art of attention.

Samuel Johnson

There were other related problem areas that required accommodation. Dr. Peterson had told Luis that I might have trouble with orientation. When I returned home, I often and without explanation, got lost, even in the most familiar of places.

My first stark recognition of this was when I visited my father and his wife in their home in Florida a few years later. One night we went out to eat. It was a nice restaurant, casual. Pat and Dad not only knew where to find the best of foods, but were always on friendly terms with the servers.

"What'll you have Carol?" Dad asked.

"I've never been here before, so what's good?"

"Well, it's Italian. We like lasagna the best."

"Great! I love lasagna!" and I ordered.

The food really was quite good, and spiced well, just the way I liked it. I drank quite a bit of water as they sipped their wine.

Eventually, Nature called and I excused myself.

"Excuse me, but, where are the bathrooms?" I asked a waitress.

"Oh, just go to the back of the restaurant, slip past the bar and take a left. The bathroom will be down the hall on the right."

Just before going, I slipped my pillbox out of my pocket. I always carried my medications to take with meals, but hidden in my pocket or purse, so that no one would notice.

I arrived at my destination without mishap. Finishing up, I left the bathroom and turned right. Reaching the end of the hallway, I came back and suddenly realized I wasn't sure which way to go. I made a guess and found myself at a dead end. I turned around and wandered back until I could hear voices at the bar. Heading in that direction, I cursed myself for being stupid enough to lose my way. Entering the restaurant, I looked around to find the table and spied Pat and Dad in the corner across the room.

By the time I reached their table, I was embarrassed.

"Where have you been? "my father laughed, "Did you take the scenic route?"

I felt awkward and tried to join in the laughter, "You'd think so, huh?"

Noting my expression, Pat brushed her hand across his arm, "Oh, stop it, Fred," she admonished.

Then, turning to me, she successfully righted the situation," Carol, you know him! Always trying to make a joke!" This was the first time I realized so pointedly, that my orientation was seriously compromised.

CHAPTER 29
Caring

People will forget what you said, people will forget
what you did, but people will never forget how you
made them feel.

Maya Angelou

There followed other times when I lost track, much to my embarrassment, and sometimes with friends or at work.

I was driving to a friends house one day and forgot the directions she had given me.

"Jenny, sorry I'm late. I forgot the directions you gave me and had some trouble finding your house."

"That's OK, Carol," she replied.

Months went by before I visited again. That was too long an interval of time to pass for me to remember how to find her house. So, I got lost and was late again.

Jen, I'm sorry to be late again."

Fortunately, Jenny was one of the few kind souls who carted me to work after the seizures. I was embarrassed to be so dependent, but neither Jim, Stacy, Kerry, Jonathan, Laura or Steve ever acted as if I were a burden. No questions were asked and no assumptions made. So I felt safe telling Jenny about my orientation problems.

"Oh, Carol, don't be silly! Just ask me next time. It's not a problem."

This gave me just what I needed to get over yet another of the many mistakes which constantly plagued me. I could forgive myself. Because I was more relaxed, it was much easier to remember the next time. I jotted down the directions to her house and slipped them securely into the glove compartment, along with the others.

However there were times when getting lost was more serious, more intimidating for Luis.

CHAPTER 30

Rescue

We must accept finite disappointment, but never lose infinite hope.

Martin Luther King Jr.

In times of trouble, a friend is recognized.

Irish Proverb

"Sorry I'm late, Luis! The traffic out of Oakland was really heavy."

This was only half the truth. I was lost on the route I had driven countless times over the years, including to attend monthly meetings at the HMO headquarters with other Behavioral Medicine managers. This was to be my last meeting as a Behavioral Medicine Subchief, before I formally stepped down from the position.

I missed my exit on the way down to the meeting, was momentarily angry with myself, then relaxed. Only because I had lived in Oakland for years before moving to Santa Rosa, did I remember how to take the next exit and backtrack.

When the meeting was over, I figured I would get home without any problem. It was rush-hour, so I stayed on the city streets, intending to meander around a while, then get back on the highway at a point where I hoped the traffic might be less.

After several more wrong turns, I saw the Oakland Children's Hospital on my right and realized I was way off course.

"Stupid, stupid, stupid!" ran the familiar litany in my head.

By the time I got my bearings, the traffic was at its thickest. I merged onto the highway and crawled ahead like an inchworm on a rainy day.

I called Luis periodically throughout the afternoon as I trudged home.

"Hi honey. There's a lot of traffic, so I'll probably be late. I'll keep you posted." I didn't mention that losing my way was the reason for my tardiness.

I never asked him if he knew what was really happening. If he did, then he knew I was an idiot, and I couldn't risk that! No, I'd rather keep pretending, being pissed off at the traffic or, if necessary, at myself!

Luis remained oblivious to my orientation problems until we went on a weekend outing. I was to meet him in Walnut Creek after work. Again, I got off at the wrong exit, recovered quickly, and merged back onto the highway.

Later, he met me at the hotel. Over dinner, we planned our next day's adventure-- mountainbiking in nearby Briones Regional Park. We loved this park, as there were so many singletrack trails with options for every level of mountainbiker. And, best of all, no cars!

Next morning, well-rested and eager to go, we loaded the bikes onto the truck after wheeling them down from our room, and drove to the Park entrance. Mountainbike tracks mixed with hiking bootprints and horse droppings crisscrossed the "parking lot," which was little more then an open field, pounded into hardpacked dirt by cars, trucks and bikes.

We mounted our bikes and began the climb up one of many singletrack trails, which meandered off in various directions. We agreed to set our own pace, checking in with each other whenever we reached one of several summits, then descending again to the lot.

Things went well – at first.

The rolling hills were familiar. The views were wonderful on that Sunday, our bodies responding well to the exercise. As always when outdoors like this together, our hearts are full and, oh, so very grateful. We separated eventually, my pace being different from his that day.

I climbed a particularly steep section of the trail, then took some time to soak in the beauty of the Park reservoir. Glancing at the time, I decided to head back by a different route as we'd been separated for a while and I didn't want to chance making him wait too long.

Big mistake.

An hour later, having made similar decisions at the crossroads of various trails, I chastised myself that I was, once again, terribly lost.

"Good grief, not again!"

I retraced my steps to the summit, the view no longer as impressive as it was frightening. Dozens of trails crisscrossed the hillsides, none of which looked familiar. I couldn't figure out how this had happened. I was confused and spiraled into my old friend, denial. Very soon though, I had to admit that I had no idea where I was.

Suddenly, it dawned on me. We were supposed to meet at the agreed upon time back at the start. All I could picture was my Luis, waiting at the entrance, checking and rechecking his watch, scanning the ridge for any sign of me, as his fear mounted. He'd probably take off searching along different routes, only to return, alone, to the empty rendezvous point. Having been there before, he'd worry that I didn't (or wasn't able to) call for help. He would be terrified and my actions, responsible.

I ascended, once again, to the top, composed myself and took yet another 360° surveillance of my surroundings. Descending, I caught a glimpse of him far across in the next valley. This image was accompanied by echoes of him frantically calling my name.

"Carol! Carol, where are you?!"

Anxious, I yelled as loud as I could, "Luis! Don't worry! I'm fine! I'm up here!"

But it was no use. My imploring reached the turkey vultures above, the squirrels scampering amongst the rocks, but not my poor husband. There was no trail leading directly into the valley where he rode, and the incline was rocky and steep.

I remembered the warning Dr. Peterson had given to Luis, "If she falls and hits her head again, that's it; no second chances."

I retraced my steps, steering as clear as I could of those steep descents and always choosing the eastern route to where Luis was anxiously waiting.

"Stupid, stupid, stupid!" I criticized myself, as anger shielded me from the fear that was wrapping around my throat.

This time, ignoring the trails, I careened through fields, across creeks and around boulders, generally moving east.

An hour later, I returned to the parking lot. He was there, pacing back-and-forth.

When he saw me, "Carol! What happened?!"

He wrapped his arms around me as I collapsed into them.

"Oh, I'm so sorry, Honey! I got to the top and just went down the wrong way."

Again, only part of the truth.

"Never mind," he consoled, "It's alright. You're here now."

He recovered quickly, to his credit, though the look on his face stayed with me long after the bikeride ended.

We loaded the bikes onto the truck and headed for home, my car following his. He shifted our positions as we drove. I knew he was riding behind me so that he could watch for and prevent further mishaps.

That night, as we laid down to sleep, the migraine descended once again.

The pain medication worked, but only after an hour of pacing in the other room.

The last words I remember thinking before I lay down again were, "Carol, you're such an idiot! How could you do that to him? Stupid, stupid, stupid!"

Subsequent to that adventure, I decided to dispense with mountainbiking as well, limiting rides to casual circumstances with Luis on a bike trail or with plenty of others. We never again rode bikes other than the "klunkers." These were large bikes Luis collected from where he worked. The refinery covered many acres of land, so the bikes were to be used as a mode of transportation. But, the idea never caught on and the bikes were left out to rust in the rain. Luis brought them home and resurrected them.

One day, we were riding a 60 mile benefit ride astride our klunkers. I was riding a ways ahead of Luis, each of us caught up in conversations with friends.

Suddenly, I toppled over into a pile of leaves by the side of the road.

I will always remember Jeff, a knight in shining armor (only this hero's steed was a bicycle) who stopped and hunkered down with me, telling someone to dial 911.

I was conscious and recovering by the time the ambulance arrived. Later, when I consulted with my neurologist, he told me that the seizure would have happened anyway, regardless of what I was doing. There was now available a prescription used for a different purpose, but found to be very effective for preventing seizures and reliable at this new point in my recovery. He periodically monitored blood levels to assure coverage, leaving me grateful (for the umpteenth time!) to the medical community and for being born late enough to benefit from such diligent research!

I was embarrassed afterwards, and felt foolish. But, Jeff did not treat me as I felt. He knew that this injury was related to the past, but continued to treat me as he always had. I was not merely a person to pity.

I learned to accommodate to the permanent shifts with that same support that encouraged me to believe in myself, to trust that I would adapt. I was greatly relieved, over time, that the change in medications was effective. There had been no more seizures and I was religious about completing the labwork necessary to assure that levels were adequate and efficacious. Several years passed without incident, and I returned to being active once again.

Luis and I agreed that to never be active in the outdoors again, would mean not fully living. That, along with my friend, Jim, is how we came to the conclusion--running was the natural choice for me. I kept my feet on the ground and off the streets, from then on.

CHAPTER 31

Powerful Words

Self-respect is the cornerstone of all virtue.

John Herschel

Brains require caring more than caring requires brains.

From Mothers and Others, by Sarah Blaffer Hrdy

At times, our own light goes out and is rekindled by a spark from another person. Each of us has cause to think with deep gratitude of those who have lighted the flame within us.

Albert Schweitzer

As I have said, once home again, I was often referred to as, "Carol, the one with the traumatic brain injury." That is to say, I was irreparably damaged. Some meant to make things easier for me, were trying to help me believe that I could recover and improve.

Others were determined that I would see how things had changed, how inept I'd become, now shackled to their diagnosis of "TBI." These people must have lacked in a medical understanding of the injury or their empathy was limited. They couldn't possibly have been aware of the enormous effort required of me to perform well, nor how much I would have had to offer because of what happened to me, were I not hobbled by their inalterable conclusions. It dawned on me the irony of how emotional pain eclipsed the physical at times.

Unfortunately, I quite often accepted what was implied and began chastising myself, as you've read. I knew I didn't have the memory I'd had before, and nearly surrendered to the thought that I would never be 'smart' again. Thank goodness, some were reassuring in expressing their observations to the contrary.

Though a psychotherapist myself, I don't know why I didn't seek psychotherapy services earlier. Eventually, years after the injury occurred, I decided to do so, but only because I'd learned, along my career path, that the experience of trauma is best processed in this way.

Unfortunately, the first attempt did not go well. One therapist (ironically) was forgetful. She forgot that I'd had a brain injury. I was (if nicely put) incredulous.

Finally, I reached out to someone who was herself a therapist. I could not see her for treatment as I knew her personally, but I trusted her judgment and respected her. She was shocked when I told her that I had not been treated by therapist since the injury occurred.

"What do you mean, Carol?! You haven't tried to find anyone you could work with?!" She sounded worried.

I knew, from the sound of her voice and because of the true professional she was, that she meant well and hoped to offer something to help me. Inwardly, I cheered. Brain injured people were so often considered to be incapable of having insight enough to engage in psychotherapy. She clearly was thinking "outside the box." She approved of the second psychotherapist I had chosen.

This therapist specialized in a technique called Eye Movement Desensitivation and Reprocessing (EMDR), most often used in the treatment of post traumatic stress disorder (PTSD). EMDR helps to process traumatic events leading to PTSD. Eventually, with treatment, these events can be recalled, though without the disabling emotional component.

Unfortunately, that particular treatment did not help. I had no memory of the actual event with which to work, as I was unconscious upon impact. Instead, we were much more successful in tackling what I considered to be deeper and more painful issues. These were my identity and my self-recrimination for being so ignorant.

"You need to stop calling yourself stupid. You're not." said my psychotherapist.

"But I know I am, Jon. I can't handle stress as well, and I can't remember like I used to."

"Good grief, Carol. Not everyone can get into Dartmouth!"

"Well, that was then and this is now. It's all different. It takes so much effort, checking and rechecking just to be sure I don't make a mistake. The only time I'm completely comfortable and focused is when I'm actually seeing a patient. Having to focus on one thing only in the moment, I do well. I know I have something worthwhile to give. Of course, it helps that we have a photo of nearly every patient in their chart! Otherwise, I might not recognize the face of someone, even if I'd seen before, but for only a short time."

I continued, "I take notes while meeting with my patients, but I never had to take any during the treatment session before. I know, from personal experience, how it feels when your therapist forgets something you've told her."

"Carol, everybody forgets things. I know I do."

"Yes, Jon, but it's normal at your age to be more forgetful. It's not, so much, at mine. I'm scared that I'll mess up. Like I said, it's so humiliating! Maybe they're right anyway. How frustrating it must be to interact with me, to have to repeat things, then feel like what I answer is worthless anyway! I pity those whose job it is to keep track of my schedule and paycheck, not to mention the Communications (operators) department. They answer and refer calls for me, way beyond the time anyone else would need to memorize the phone numbers."

"Geez Carol, thanks, I get it. Now, let's talk about how you survive. Think of something positive in your interactions with others," he suggested.

I thought for a minute, then, with a sigh of relief, I told him, "Frankly, I've been amazed by the staff on the module where I work. They've created a family-like atmosphere there. They even call one woman,

'Mom!' Have you ever heard of that before in a work setting?! They can get really mad at each other sometimes, but, when push comes to shove, they've got each others' backs, mine included. I think that might be the reason I was placed there when I got back--less stress and support guaranteed."

After that session, though I still felt 'less than,' at least there was the occasional question mark (instead of exclamation point) at the end of my predictable comment about myself.

When this therapist died, I, too, grieved. What a gift he'd been to the field, also invaluable to me.

Once again despairing, I called my neurologist and asked whether these memory problems would ever stop.

"Carol, the very fact that you remember that you forget, is testament to having memory," John replied.

Such interactions buoyed me with the possibility that some others, at least, saw me as more than just someone who had suffered a traumatic brain injury. Supportive friends, especially those who show you the respect of accepting your help in return, are crucial to find.

The same held true for some health providers whose 'bedside manner' complimented their stellar medical acumen. I advise others to look for those who, first and foremost, take their time with you as much as is reasonable.

It helped me to take a list of my concerns, the more specific and reviewed beforehand, the better. None of the doctors could spend an hour with me, of course, but the time with him or her in the appointment room was much more productive if I did my homework.

Fortunately, the several neurologists who followed me during the years afterwards (including the one I saw only a little while before he retired) were open and responsive.

Say what you will (and I know I'm biased) about HMO's, but mine sure did right by me.

One of my neurologists was outside my HMO. He was referred to me directly by the neurosurgeon. This neurologist, Dr. Sherwood, was the very doctor who kept me doggedly listening to my body, "You can run distance runs, but always, always stay hydrated."

If only I had listened sooner!

He always began the appointment with a question, rather than hurrying immediately into standard functional testing.

"So, how're you doing nowadays? Any particular concerns?"

I was free to launch into a summary of my symptoms, having looked forward to our conversation. He listened carefully, respectfully, before responding.

"Some good days, some bad," I began, in response to his question. "Still have the migraines, of course. I know I'll have them the rest of my life, but it's these memory lags that plague me most of all! Some days, it might be easier to crawl under a rock, just disappear for a while. I wish there was something that would help!"

"Carol, you need to let up on yourself. You went through major trauma and are doing so incredibly well. There are bound to be some problems, but your cognitive functioning is not bad. You make it worse by criticizing yourself."

I confess that I hoped to hear such words and this was one reason, in and of itself, that I looked forward to seeing him. I wasn't as stupid as I thought. I was working and had done so since only several months after brain surgery and for years since then.

That having been emphasized, he asked if I was still taking Topamax to prevent migraines.

"Yea, but it's not helping," I replied.

He advised that this medication could contribute to memory problems and that there were others I might try. I contacted my HMO neurologist who agreed that this made sense and worked with me to come up with an alternative to try, in the hope that the memory problems would be less deflating.

Dr. Sherwood continued, next addressing my other concern--the migraines.

"Last time we met, you were having them four or five times a week. Did you happen to try the Botox injections I suggested?"

He had been encouraging me to try Botox, knowing others experienced some relief from the treatment, when all else seemed to fail.

I hesitated, but figured he, if anyone, would understand my resistance.

"Doctor, even the thought of sticking needles anywhere in my head, even away from the area of the head trauma, is just a little too scary for me."

He continued to suggest it every so often, always gently and understanding my fear. Only those times when I was having them four and five times a week, would he mention it again as an option. His persistent delivery of the message (always coupled with respect for my fear) finally convinced me to give it a try.

Unfortunately, the migraines continued, but I knew I probably didn't give it a sufficient number of sessions. The fear was simply too much for me, and he understood.

But, I appreciated the referral in the end. By that time, I was open to trying whatever treatment was available. I had faced my opponent in the ring and fought a respectable round. Though I didn't win that fight, I defeated much greater foes--my fears of the unknown and of losing hope that I would ever find some relief.

Next, I gave biofeedback a try. Through the use of a monitoring device, I was able to consciously lower my blood pressure. Unfortunately, focusing on any screen eventually triggered a migraine.

Nevertheless, because of engaging in the treatment, I was open to searching for another possible option.

Over time, I felt more and more burdened by the pain. I dispensed with the meditation I had practiced for twenty years, except for the related practice of yoga. Biofeedback gave me the assurance I needed, in order to voluntarily control a bodily sensation (blood pressure). Meditation, using that same focus, allowed me to separate myself from the pain for a time and, instead, appreciate the healthier parts of my body. By breathing into each part of my body, head to toe (i.e., doing a "body scan") I was no longer thoroughly absorbed in pain. This focus, in and of itself, consciously reduced the stress which could trigger a migraine.

As I've mentioned, I was extremely fortunate in my choice of personal physicians at my HMO.

One morning in the parking garage, I was walking from my car out of the lot. Two women hailed me and asked how I was doing. Maryann was a nurse practitioner who had been my gynecology provider for years. The other woman was a friend of hers, Anita, also in the OB/GYN department. I hadn't seen Anita in quite a while. Both of them were quite friendly and knew me well, so I felt awkward about not remembering Anita's face. They were so nice that I felt safe enough to tell them how embarrassed I was and why. I even went so far as to explain why I never told anyone. They couldn't possibly have been more understanding and were refreshingly brief in their reassurances, as though anyone could feel that way in my position. That was it, no more discussion about that, just on to everyday things. They couldn't possibly have known how much I'd appreciated being treated as "normal."

When John Cassidy (my operatic doc) retired, I had to choose another neurologist at my HMO (continuing with Dr. Sherwood for the periodic appointment). The Neurology medical assistants suggested Dr. Gilbert. Indeed, she afforded not only excellent medical care, but validation to boot.

Early on, I sent her an email regarding frustration with my memory and asked what she might suggest. I explained that the loss of some cognitive function left me feeling inferior.

She quickly messaged me back, "Hi Carol. Despite your history of traumatic brain injury and history of seizures, I continue to be amazed at how much you can do. Furthermore, you have been working and performing your job duties without difficulty -- this requires lots of cognitive skills. I think this is the strongest evidence that you are doing well."

I held onto that one for years.

As I said, stellar service, coupled with empathy, goes a long way toward influencing healing. Here, the added touch of kind words, kept me going when times got rough.

And, then, there was my amazingly dedicated primary care physician (yes, one and the same) Dr. David Pastran. He tolerated the little poems I composed in messaging him, sometimes responding in rhyme himself. Yup, a sense of humor is an invaluable gift to patients at times!

Bless him, he taught me another lesson which, like hydration, I had to learn the hard way.

"David, I'm concerned again. I saw the results of my lab tests and something looks off," I emailed him, "Would you take a look and get back to me?"

He followed up with a call (which he frequently did after hours, I might add), "Carol, we've been through this before. Nothing to worry about--really. The levels go up and down, but it's normal for you and nothing to worry about."

I tried to backpedal, "Sorry. I just freaked out; you know how I am."

"Well, how 'bout you take notes this time? I mean, with the memory problems, you think it might help?" he asked.

"Geez," I thought. I was forever encouraging others to take pen to paper and say aloud what they wanted to remember. So, I really couldn't use the excuse, "Sorry, I forgot."

"Yup, you got me. Just a sec, I'll write it down."

As expected, he laughed along with me. (Some doctors are exemplary. Empathy and compassion are not learned in school, now are they?)

"Good!" I was so glad that he had reminded me in such a nice way. Instead of getting mad at myself as usual, I could focus on how I had created some solutions to the problem.

There were other contributions such as these, to challenge my eternal damnation and which, though my memory was worse, I could never forget. These affirmations of hope were like sunrises, more and more triumphant over the sunsets of despair.

Still, it was years before I was told something which helped me to realize that I was not as unintelligent as I thought, as some implied.

While rehabilitating at John Muir after the injury, I was given a battery of neuropsychological tests. These revealed that some of my cognitive capacities were not at the same level as before.

I never looked at that report until years later, just as I did not read much about the brain (though I bought books to read, later, if I felt more comfortable).

Once again, in 2009, I went through a battery of neuropsychological tests.

When I received the results, I was overjoyed! Regardless of what I was lead to believe, progress had been made. I improved in, or maintained at previous level, most cognitive skills.

"The patient performed Within Expectations in most areas of cognitive functioning (Attention/mental tracking, language functioning, visuospatial/constructional functioning complex visual – motor sequencing, verbal memory, visual recognition memory, and executive functioning) and demonstrates significant improvements in most areas since her prior examination in 2006."

Several distinct comments stayed with me:

"These scores suggest an improvement in her visual spatial memory performance since 2006."

"The skills were all improved from a prior performance."

"Actually improved on visual divided attention."

I was not surprised (and it was affirming in any case) that anxiety and depression significantly impacted my cognitive performance. It was also noted on the test:

"The clinical interview was conducted to assess for the presence or absence of a psychiatric disturbance. The patient denied any symptoms of a mood or thought disorder. However, she admits to some anxiety and this was evident during the examination. Her Beck Depression Inventory – 2 score was 16 which suggests that she is experiencing mild depressive symptoms at this time."

"Her mood currently appears stable but she endorses mild depressive symptoms and her anxiety appears to negatively affect her performance. Given the severity of her TBI, she has really made quite a remarkable recovery and has successfully maintained her employment status."

"Well," I thought, "memory, alone, does not define intelligence." Good to know.

The most encouraging and validating of all, were the results of the IQ test:

"Selected subtests of the WAIS-3 were administered as measures of estimated pre-morbid general cognitive functioning. On this administration, her estimated I Q values fell in at least the High Average to superior range. Her scores appeared generally consistent with her estimated pre- morbid level of functioning based on her education and occupation."

Based on my experience then, when supported by kind words from others (be they friends, medical providers, family, or a mixture of these) I felt brave enough to assert myself, to make a choice in my care. These folks were just the sunglasses I needed to reduce the blinding glare of self-doubt, enough to access the level of confidence and self esteem I once had.

CHAPTER 32
Bag O'Tricks

All the world is full of suffering. It is also full of overcoming.

Helen Keller

Never let the fear of striking out get in your way.

Babe Ruth

Set aside some regular daily quiet time. If convenient, agree with a few like-minded friends to spend a minimum of fifteen minutes a day. Teach yourself how to quiet the body, and how to empty the mind.

Lewis M. Stevens (my grandfather, who, in attitude, elocution, and action, was a man way ahead of his time).

Some days, I felt as if I were wearing boots of granite, such a struggle was it to walk along the road I needed to travel. Fortunately, there were also dates on my calendar that turned as if on a breath of fresh air. These were the days I successfully conquered dismay about what I considered to be my deficiencies.

Over time, especially when encouraged, I developed a number of "tricks" to help me surmount obstacles others seldom encountered. Some, I retained and carried over from my previous life, while others, I developed to supplement my limitations.

I have already mentioned some of these helpful "tricks", and you will discover your own. (e.g. jotting down the name of a person I just met, along with a particular feature of that person, then keeping it in my car as a reference for the our next expected meeting). I repeat some here for emphasis (or in case you are short on time and skipped to this part of the book first!). Some are valuable relaxation techniques, while others help to enhance or assist memory. Still others are ways I used to remind and motivate myself. I found that making habits out of such simple techniques doubled their efficacy.

Jon Kabat Zinn published <u>Full Catastrophe Living</u> (Random House, 1990). This work served to guide me, as I waded into mindfulness meditation. Soon, he wrote another--<u>Wherever You Go, There You Are</u> (Hatchette Books, 2005). More recently I discovered, <u>The Mindful Path to Self-Compassion</u>, by Christopher K. Germer (Guilford Press, 2009). These books grounded me in the principles necessary to develop and return to a daily morning meditation practice and convinced me of the benefits possible.

During those early years, I also established a morning routine. Never having developed a hankering for caffeine, I explained my routine to friends who were interested in learning more about how I kickstarted my day. Half an hour of what I called "meditation in motion" (yoga) followed by fifteen minutes of sitting mindfully, substituted for a cup of coffee in the morning.

Beginning with increased awareness through mindfulness, I grew more alert and responsive through movement, rather than to fall asleep while relaxing. Each activity involved focusing on the breath as I began my day. Then followed whatever aerobic exercise I was enjoying at the time.

When I came out of the coma, I was unable to move much. So, I continued these practices in the only way I could. I had read somewhere that my body would respond to the mere thought of doing the yoga exercises I'd done every morning for years.

But, in time, I felt the need to develop some new routines as accommodation to changes. Our friend, Steve, suggested that I carry a small spiral notebook to record what I wanted to remember. Seems a rather simple thing, but, at the time, it was a lifesaver. Each day, I collected my small notebook, filled with a list of "things to do," and my calendar of events and activities. I also gathered insights to review and sustain myself along the road to self confidence.

It was a morale builder to have these with me at all times. While others were programming their iPhones, I preferred having a pen and paper in hand. I was injured just as iphones were becoming ubiquitous and I hadn't had time enough to adapt. Changing horses in the middle of a fast-moving stream of changes, seemed unnecessary and potentially disastrous.

Oddly enough, it was now easier than before to focus on only one thing intensely at a time (such as the patient I was treating) rather than to be distracted by the multitude of changes with which I was bombarded outside my office. Practicing psychotherapy afforded me the opportunity to help patients with a new level of empathy-- "living in the moment," if you will, when providing treatment. This facility bespoke my adherence to walking respectfully with a patient as they struggled, and accomplished, access to the solutions lying within themselves.

I kept as much to routine as I could during the day, in order to reduce interruption or distraction from this process. My glasses were always hung at my collar when I was not wearing them. Notes for each session were carefully placed in chronological order on my desk, to be completed during the first half of the lunch hour. I reorganized my office so that I could establish habits to keep things running smoothly and without much effort, on my part.

The books I most often used as resources, I kept on my office bookshelf in order of type (anxiety, depression, chemical dependency, abuse, the mind/body connection, etc.), titles facing out. I recommended them and encouraged patients to peruse my copy briefly toward the end of the session. If the patient felt it might be helpful, he/she borrowed it from the library or bought one.

Once the patient completed reviewing a book or article, I set it aside and returned it to the bookcase in its original position, following the session. If I loaned a book, I always put a note with the date it was loaned inconspicuously under the book next to it. That way, I could easily check on the date and the first name (only) of the patient who borrowed it. I would check my past schedule and give them a ring if I needed it.

Luis was the first one to notice that too much time in front of the computer screen, could lead to a migraine. There was a threshold beyond which, if I continued, I would feel a migraine coming on while still at work or by the time I got home.

One evening, several hours after the close of the clinic, I returned home. I typically clocked in at least a few extra hours a day, some before, some after work. I didn't see anything wrong with this. I was used to it, and many of the doctors (if not all) did the same.

"Carol, it's so late. Were you writing notes for so long after work again?" Luis asked when I returned home even later than usual.

I shrugged, "OK, I did it again. Sorry," as the telltale signs of the pain militia pressed upward toward the border of my skull.

"Look, hon', we both already know they're worse when you're most frustrated or depressed, but some of it might also be that damn computer!"

The next day I approached my module manager, "Tony, these headaches seem to be getting worse. Do you think an ergonomic evaluation might be in order? Also, the fluorescent lights seem to aggravate the problem. What do you think?"

"Sure, I'll put in a request," he replied.

Russ, of the I.T. Department, recommended that I give my eyes a break periodically, look away from the screen for a few minutes and focus on something else. A good friend, Pat, piggybacked this advice with a trick of her own. Every 15 minutes, she looked away for 30 seconds, again, focusing on something else. I found that removing my glasses enhanced the effect. Writing this book would not have been possible, were it not for such people, their empathy and suggestions.

These minor adjustments made quite a difference in the number and intensity of the migraines. This experience was a chance for me to learn how to ask for help, without the ever present risk of embarrassment.

There were other tricks of the trade I gathered over the years.

Another problem was that I could not, for the life of me, remember where I'd placed items I'd laid down only moments before. I forgot whether I'd turned off the heating pad I'd used for a sore muscle while reading in another room, before going to bed, and whether I'd already called my good friend to wish her a Happy Birthday (or if, in fact, it actually was her birthday!). (Facebook has solved that problem, as you likely know, by sending out reminders of birthdays!)

These things would not have been problematic if, like everyone else, they happened only occasionally. Unfortunately, they were quite common occurrences for me.

If I put my glasses or another item in a place other than I customarily did, I tended to forget where I had put them. Other people might do this as is typical of growing older. However, I misplaced things much more than would be expected at my age.

So, whenever I placed my glasses on top of the washer while loading laundry, or put my watch on the shelf while doing the dishes, I said aloud where I'd placed them. All the more effective if I said it more than once.

I had a much better chance of remembering this change in routine if, added to this, I wrote down any shift in the usual pattern. I used the same technique for remembering faces, directions, and where I parked the car or the location of a lunch hour meeting.

I already explained how memory problems in everyday situations, could be cumbersome at best. I was initially very frustrated that I had to review what I'd read only the day before, prior to moving on to the next chapter of the book. That was until I discovered that if I jotted down a few notes during or just after I stopped reading, I had much better retention. This was true whether or not I looked at the notes again. I kept this a secret from my book club members for years, afraid of being embarrassed as a result.

As it turned out, this was unfair. Eventually when I confided in some of them, they chuckled in response.

One confessed, "Carol, sometimes when I don't have time to read the book, I just look over summaries online before the next time we meet!"

Similar 'tricks' I've described for remembering faces and names. If I spoke someone's name aloud seven times after meeting them for the first time, simultaneously picturing a specific aspect of their face or body, this improved my recall.

The Memory Bible (2002), by Dr. Gary Small, MD, offered many such hints. I was lucky enough to be in contact with a brilliant physician, Dr. Wynn Canio, who trained with him at the UCLA Longevity Center. She introduced me to the book which described what was a new technique to me at the time, "Look, Snap, Connect." I took to it immediately because It reminded me of the way I had learned to speak French in college, from Dr. John Rassias.

Dr. Rassias was a renowned professor and language teacher. He developed a process for learning a new language, using the demands "Snap, Point, Look," while simultaneously pointing and moving directly toward the student. Sometimes, this somewhat portly man would actually leap up on a chair in order to accent the phrase he was after. I am not sure whether he did so in every class he taught, many being overseas at the invitation of institutions in other countries. I do know he made learning that much more effective for me and for the many thousands of Peace Corps volunteers who learned through his process. He died in 2015 at the ripe old age of 90. (All of that jumping around doesn't seem to have hurt him, now does it)?

Because of this experience in college, I was even better prepared to learn and incorporate Dr. Small's technique.

When he was planning a meal, Luis often asked me, "Honey, would you pick up a few things at the store for me?"

"Sure, hon'. What do you need?"

"Just some grapes, a head of lettuce, a bottle of milk and a few apples. Do you want me to write it down for you?"

After a moment of thought, "Nope, I think I've got it."

I quickly composed a sentence or phrase using the first letter of each item.

"Grab Linda's Mighty Arms," for grapes, lettuce, milk, apples.

Eventually, I grew more adept at having each word sound more like the actual item.

"Seriously (cereal), egzactly (eggs), what (bottled water), applies (apples)?" It became a game, thus making it more memorable.

These little machinations not only decreased disagreements or accusations of not paying attention; they also afforded me a sense of empowerment. I began, in fact, to share some of these little bright spots with some of my patients.

"Megan, how do you teach your daughter to remember things?" I asked of a patient who had had a stroke and was only 30 years old. She was enormously frustrated with her difficulty remembering. She was still quite bright and, thus, more confounded by the event and the changes resulting from it.

"How do you help your daughter remember things?"

"Well, I usually make it into a game – a song or something." she explained.

"Like? "I asked.

You know, like the ABC song."

"So, singing it with her helps? "I asked.

"Yes."

"Then what?"

"I tell her she must be so proud of herself!"

"Does she remember?" I asked.

"Usually, after we sing it a few times. "she told me.

"So, making it into a game, practicing with someone else, congratulating her, and repeating it aloud many times, seems to work. How can you do the same for yourself?" I asked.

Based on this template, she developed a version of this plan to use for herself.

Days like this, I tried to focus on what I was learning about myself in the process of helping others. Just as most people do, I felt most fulfilled when I was able to help.

Sometimes, however, it was not possible to reach that point regarding those in need.

CHAPTER 33
Homeless

Material and physical suffering is suffering from hunger, from homelessness, from all kinds of diseases. But the greatest suffering is being lonely, feeling unloved, having no one. I have come more and more to realize that it is being unwanted that is the worst disease that any human being can ever experience."

Mother Teresa

Some days, despite my best efforts, I didn't feel as productive as I wanted. It was on one such day that I discovered a place I could go during the lunch hour, just to be alone and rejuvenate.

Walking beneath the redwoods along the perimeter of the hospital to the north and the south, I noticed a tiny dirt path stemming from the back entrance and curving around, then running parallel to the highway. My break at the noon hour was never really a "lunch hour," anyway. I scrambled to complete notes and tried to keep to my resolve to go outside for half an hour. When it was not possible both to complete notes and finish my lunch, I carried my lunch container and a set of the ever ready chopsticks to use while eating as I walked.

The weather had been particularly inclement when I headed out on my daily constitutional one day. As I ambled down the path, I noticed a bundle of clothes and a plastic bag, settled atop a heating vent of some sort. The first day I saw it, I just walked by. The path terminated at a manhole cover, where I composed myself, sang a few refrains of a song, then retraced my steps. I wondered about what I'd seen, but decided not to mention it to anyone.

Next day, as I walked along the path, I spied a leg coming out from under the jumble. A homeless man was lying amongst the rags, sound asleep. I was distressed to think that someone could be relegated to such a desperate form of existence.

When I volunteered at Juvenile Hall, I met young people who were homeless, at least for a part of their lives. I asked one young man why he continued the same behavior a dozen times, since he knew this would result in him being returned to the Hall. He told me he felt "safe here." Now, I understood more fully. Some boys and girls had parents who were either absent or drug-addicted. These kids joined gangs, seeking a 'family' of their own, and often began to deal or use drugs or vandalize. They were "safer" in the Hall. They were fed three times a day and had a place to sleep where opposing gang members were unable to confront them.

Some of the them revered the officers who served as positive role models, even considered the possibility that they might someday become an officer themselves.

One young man told me, "I've been there, so I figure I know better than they do what these guys need."

I "figured" he might be right!

Maybe this man, too, was escaping such tragedy, either in adulthood or as a child. Or, maybe, he was coping with a mental illness, lacking funds or the will, to be treated. I figured he was a temporary resident and was doing no harm, only using the vent for a place to sleep at night. I returned the next day, peering ahead to make sure he was not there.

I guess, looking back, that I might have had reason to be afraid. Once again, anger (this time in someone else's behalf) at his situation came to my rescue and I continued, without fear.

The next day, there he was again, and I thought it wise not to get too close. I came within about 20 yards, then turned around.

This became my daily routine. When he was absent, I would go to the end of the trail before turning back. I considered leaving something inconspicuous by the vent or the sleeping bag. I didn't want to leave anything too significant, knowing that he might be afraid I'd reported his existence. All I could think about was how determined a soul must be to continue living in such a way.

One day I noticed he was not there. His bundles, too, were missing.

My first thought was that someone on the Kaiser construction crew had seen him and had "evicted" him, from the only place he knew as home now. I kept an eye out for his return, day after day and, finally, there he was – his arm sprawled out from underneath the dilapidated sleeping bag.

That's when I realized. Whatever pride and respect I had lost, I still had people in my life who loved me and would never let me get to this point, who would help. Friends and family and Luis never failed me. This man was not as fortunate, and he taught me a valuable lesson. I can only hope that he survived and found someone in his life as loving as I had.

CHAPTER 34
Housefire

The road to success is always under construction.

Lily Tomlin

Several years later, we had a housefire. We'd placed the coals from the fireplace, into a metal bucket which sat outside overnight. Luis, as usual, stuck his hand into the ashes to be sure they were completely cool, then deposited the remains into the garbage bin. Unfortunately, an imperceptible coal, lying fallow overnight, ignited the few inconspicuous dry leaves lying in the bottom of the can. The latent embers sparked into flame whilst we obliviously paddled nearby on Spring Lake.

Cathy (a neighbor across the street) called 911 when she saw the fire devouring the garage. Our neighbors next door (Ray and Becky) quickly saw what was going on, no doubt even more concerned as they'd had a new baby just weeks before.

By the time help arrived, Ray's fence had begun to smolder, but, luckily, was doused in the first efforts of the fire responders.

The smoke seeped into bedding, clothes and linen. Water from powerful firehouses drenched and flooded under floorboards and sinks, causing damage difficult to repair. Floor tiles had to be ripped out and replaced.

But the fire was not all trauma and loss. There were bright spots in the melee.

Friends came out of the woodwork, offering a place to stay, to share a meal, or just to spend time and lend a sympathetic ear. Somehow, it helped to know that others had survived similar circumstances. Perhaps misery really does love company, provided the burden can be lightened through understanding.

Our friend, David, went far beyond the delicious meal prepared. He introduced us to something called "Fireglass." This is a type of glass which warms up quite quickly, then emits its own warmth, just as does a woodfire, though without the flammable residue which can lead to a fire.

We counted our blessings that neither of us was hurt, knowing that material things can be replaced. But, loved ones, not so.

Speaking of blessings, Luis had some explaining to do. He had not been to church since childhood, and only then under duress.

"I survived Catholic school," is his response to anyone who asks about it.

Amazingly enough, just that week, I had finally convinced him to go with me to spend an hour with my faith community (Emmaus) which met twice a month to worship and support each other, as well as to decide where and how to impact local and world needs. Members of the congregation took turns providing the liturgy at each service as there was neither pastor nor priest. Some had left the Church because of their disdain for behaviors and policies promulgated, such as the Church's stand on homosexuality, the stricture against allowing women to become priests, and a woman's right to choose.

(Hopefully, Pope Francis is turning the tide).

I had finally convinced Luis to come with me, not only because he liked David, and (possibly more important than anything for that first visit) because there was a potluck afterwords. There was nothing quite as tempting for Luis, as the opportunity to cook a meal for others. That day, while on the lake, I reminded him of his pledge to accompany me.

Obviously, our plans had changed. Later, I told him that, should he truly not want to join me, there were easier ways and far less devastating, to accomplish the task. He responded quickly that this was actually a sign that he should never set foot in the place! Obviously, there was to be further discussion on this topic.

Before we settled down into the townhouse which was to serve as our home for the next six months (thank you, AAA) we were relegated to staying in a hotel.

Despite the negative reputation of insurance companies in certain circles, ours really stepped up to the plate. Yet another loss recovered, whole and intact, as was the steady course of my relationship with Luis and the singing I so treasured.

Within mere weeks, AAA helped us to organize and store what was left of our things not damaged by the water, fire and smoke. We settled into a nice townhouse which was next to a park with a trail running through it. Happily, this added a mile or two to my run, so I was mollified.

Unfortunately, there were some drawbacks.

The first day we arrived, the man living with his mother just across from us, busied himself all day by roaming steadily up and down the street, muttering to himself and to the invisible friend accompanying him. He periodically was annoyed by something the other person said, stood up and spewed expletives while rushing down the street.

That weekend, there was a crowd gathered in his driveway, toddlers included. Late into the night they grew louder and carried on, obviously inebriated and careless with the four kids they brought along with them. Frequent references were made to a nearby county, small sections of which are notorious for inebriation, as well as methamphetamine abuse. This, as you can imagine, colored our feelings about the neighborhood.

I told Luis that I would handle it, not to worry. I headed toward the door, planning to chastise them soundly for their behavior. (I have mentioned to some very loyal friends that, despite appearances to the contrary, I can pose a very intimidating figure--all 100 or so pounds of me).

Needless to say, Luis disagreed. He caught me just before I left the house and slammed the door.

"What the hell's the matter with you?! C'mon back in here!"

He opened the window, exasperated, and yelled, "Hey! Keep it down out there!"

They actually did simmer down for a while, but then became boisterous again until about three in the morning.

Next day, as I was backing out of residential parking, there was the unusual man chatting with his elderly mother.

Luis already off to work, I decided to pose my threatening stance once again.

"Hey, did you hear those people in your driveway last night? They were making a lot of noise, don't you think?"

No doubt I was snowing them with my subtle approach.

"No, didn't hear nothin'." he replied.

This was an unanticipated response, so I let him have it, "Well, I nearly called the police! Next time, I will!"

Quickly, I sped away in my little red car, leaving them to chuckle and point at me. Even so, I was sure they were frightened by my thinly veiled threats.

Unfortunately, I guess I was mistaken because, the very next weekend, they resumed their shenanigans.

I tried to resign myself to our situation and eventually turned my attention to yet another form of consternation in the neighborhood. I decided it was important for me to resolve the issue of small children riding around the cul-de-sac without helmets on their heads. As anyone might guess, I had a very strong opinion about protecting one's noggin.

Once again, I was certain about the outcome, that the parents would respond appreciatively when I educated them about the risk they were taking with their children's lives. After all, they were Latino families, steeped in a culture that valued the family and children. They listened, nodding politely to every caution I espoused, then returned to their homes. They may not have understood a word I said or (more likely) were merely tolerating my intrusion. The children continued to trundle around the parking lot and streets on their scooters and bikes, helmetless and content.

Thereafter, Luis increased the number of safety checks he ran on me daily. These had previously been to see if I had fallen or otherwise injured myself while running in the Park. Afterwards, he called at other times of the day, just to make sure I was not pushing the limits with our neighbors!

Next birthday, Luis confirmed his belief in recovery by gifting me with a glorious symbol of my independence--a new solo canoe to replace the one I had lost in the fire.

Early one morning, I loaded this canoe onto the car, hoisting it from the rack on the side of the house and onto the hood of the car. I drove to the lake, slid it off the car and, again onto my head. When I reached the lake, I flipped it over into the water, stepped into the seat, situated my water bottle and pushed off. Just as the motion of running incited song, so the rhythmic swing of the paddle from side to side, inspired me to open my mouth and sing!

Oh, such a glorious free feeling and, yet another affirmation that we could and were, recovering.

Once again ashore, I hesitated, the noggin a bit unsettled, perhaps unwilling to emerge from the peace and quiet solitude on the lake. Or, maybe, just maybe, I was resisting the weight of the canoe on my, now, slightly compromised crown.

As always, I ignored what I felt was interfering, shifted my weight, hoisted the canoe atop my head and turned towards the car.

Most often I made it to the car without mishap, that is, except for when a small child appeared suddenly on his bike. Riding along, carefree and well ahead of his parents, he would inevitably be oblivious to a large canoe crossing his path. These close calls taught me to be hypervigilant.

"Hey, do you need some help?" the occasional passerby would ask.

It took me a while to trust and share burdens of any kind with someone else. Most often, when asked, I would politely decline, fearing that anybody interrupting my careful 'hoist, lift, and heave' protocol, would imbalance the process, sending me and my canoe toppling onto the asphalt, and rendering me annoyed as all get out.

The offer, that day, of a well-meaning soul, along with my hesitance to begin the process, convinced me (for that day at least) to accept someone's help.

"Yes, please!" I replied, "I sure could use a hand!"

Since then, I can't remember ever being disappointed in the help offered, even if thrown off balance for a second.

"Thanks so much!" I replied.

"No problem."

Later, when Luis got home, "Hon', how'd ya get it over there? How did you manage to get it on and off the rack?" he asked, a worried look on his face.

"Not to worry, 'uigi (my nickname for him) I had some help on the other end. Some kind soul took pity on me and helped me lift it on to the car."

I knew it would happen again and that, next time, things would go more smoothly. I was learning how to trust that others would help when needed, rather than make it worse.

I thanked Luis, in the way I knew best. I created something from my heart to his:

Luis, thank you for the most thoughtful present,
Ever that I have received.
Beyond anything that I could've imagined,
If told, I would't have believed!

And with this, we finally find closure,
To a chapter of our lives filled with fear.
But our bond grows ever stronger,
With the passing of difficult years.

An injury, the first time threatened,
To take me away from you.
Then, a fire nearly destroyed our home,
The one you've made better than new.

Just now, leaving the latest behind us,
Which would've separated us if one died.
We learned once again, with dear friends' help,
That prayers are answered and love abides.

CHAPTER 35

I Always Will

Pain is the deepest thing we have in nature, and union through pain and suffering has always seemed more real and holy than any other.

Henry Hallam

I was never much for tears when tragedies happened– before. I wondered why I rarely felt the urge to sob – not following the event, nor at times when everyone cried for joy. I took it in stride, offered condolences when appropriate, and moved on.

After being injured, things changed. I cried for reasons anyone would, though the intensity might be greater than before.

Initially, people did not understand. They labelled me "reactive," "emotional," even, "paranoid." This last was particularly off-putting as, someone who is paranoid is fearful without reasonable cause. When I returned, the lack of understanding I experienced from those few, fully warranted feeling anxious and afraid that I was truly worthless.

More adroitly put, how could I not be afraid? Someone smacked into me with a car, watched me fly off my bike, then left me as I lay motionless on the ground, bleeding and unconscious, to die alone.

Still, maybe I was more emotionally expressive overall. There are some memories (now and probably forever) which will overwhelm me, regardless of the setting or who's with me at the time.

One evening quite a while after I returned home, we invited some of our favorite couples over for dinner. John and Joan were always amongst those at the top of the list. They were warm and vocally appreciative of Luis's culinary mastery, thus endearing them to him. Another of the couples was Steve and Esther (well-known to the reader by now).

We also invited Steve and Linda, a kind and thoughtful couple. They had allowed us to spend a rejuvenating weekend at their house on the bluff overlooking the ocean at Dillon Beach, and another in their trailer right on the beach.

Larry and his wife, Justine, rounded out the group, allowing us to thank them once again, for stepping up to the plate in our time of need.

Steve and Linda arrived, carrying a beautiful bouquet of flowers and some fresh crab which Steve had caught himself, to complement Luis's creations. Others joined us shortly afterwards. The couples, eyeing the food, agreed that they were in for an exceptional meal.

We enjoyed ourselves and our time together—stimulating conversations liberally peppered with hearty laughter. Luis first served fresh bread and a unique salad to precede the entree. Next, the renowned paella took centerstage. All were mesmerized by that time. The artistic dining adventure closed with a mouthwatering fruit tart—blueberries, red strawberries and bright green kiwis—a rainbow of gastronomic delight.

Luis, ever the showman, served each dish with a flourish reminiscent of the "Iron Chef," straight from the oven or stovetop and onto the table, tempting his prodigiously-salivating guests.

After the meal, the coffee could only be "Peets."

"Is there any other kind worth having?" asked the Chef.

None chose to challenge the statement. Guests and hosts leaned back in their chairs, fully sated and duly incredulous.

Someone, inadvertently—innocently—mentioned "the accident." Startled, I said nothing at first. I suddenly realized that I deplored reference to what happened to me as an "accident." After all, "accident" nearly excused the act, therefore the culpability, regardless of what followed (or didn't, in this case!)

I refrained from sharing this thought.

Every once in a while, the "memory" question was asked (such as the previous dinner with Steve and Esther at their house). "Do you remember it? I mean, that day?"

These queries were usually followed in quick succession by many others, "So, Carol, do you remember when you came to? Did you know where you were?"

"How long were you out?"

I would manage to nod sagely, share what I could, roll my eyes convincingly, then guide the conversation away from the topic.

"The whole thing was pretty crazy. Lots has changed since then, but I'm back to my old self now."

Back to myself on the surface--no tears, no expression of fear there.

I described what I could remember from just prior to the event, but had never ventured further into what happened in the hospital. I hadn't been ready to talk about the aftermath until this dinner with friends.

Steve looked at me, with a side glance at Esther, who nodded. He decided I was OK with the question and began.

"Carol, can you remember when you found out what happened?" Steve asked.

Before I responded, I turned to Luis. He sat silently, taking into account the encouraging faces around him of people he trusted entirely, then encouraged me to go on. Looking back now, I know this was the first he felt safe enough to hear and say what happened.

Once again, it helped enormously that the guests were physicians and their spouses. They were, after all, just curious and impressed by the magnitude of the injury.

My 'memories' of what happened as I regained consciousness were the stories based on Luis's trauma-inhibited recall, the gaps later bridged by others' accounts.

I proceeded to explain what details I could remember and what was told to me by others and, later, by Luis.

I lay unconscious in the I.C.U., following major surgery. My body was limp as I struggled to live--aided by the numerous tubes and monitors encircling the bed.

Luis was in the waitingroom, surrounded by our friends and family.

"Mr. Colina! Mr. Colina!"

Hearing his name and the urgency in her voice, he leaped up and ran to the nurse.

"Mr. Colina, come with me." She turned away and marched towards my room.

"Oh," she said as she turned at the door, gathering the full extent of her error. His face was hollowed, as though smashed by a boxer's mitt--a perfectly-executed punch, a knock out. He swerved, staring at her as his mouth dropped open and tears filled his eyes.

"No, no, Mr. Colina! It's O.K.! We just want you to come and see her. She's breathing on her own. The doctor thinks she can hear us! Come inside, will you?"

He did not answer--could not. Obediently and in a daze, he followed her into the room and over to the bed where I lay. He looked at me, my head entirely swathed in bandages with traces of clotted blood visible though the gauze. The nurse explained. The machines helped me to breathe, to push blood through my veins, to nourish and to deliver fluid and medicines--to keep me alive.

"Mr. Colina, stand here by the bed, next to her."

He did as he was told.

"Now," she began, "the doctor says she can hear. Take your wife's hand."

He reached towards me, gently placing his large calloused hand under my frail one--a robin's egg in her nest.

"We think she can hear," the nurse repeated, "Can we call you Luis?"

He nodded, his eyes never wavering. The nurse moved to his side.

"Carol, can you hear me?" she asked the listless body on the bed.

"Carol, this is Luis. This is your husband. He's here. He's holding your hand. Squeeze."

A choking sound erupted from Luis's throat as he leaned towards me.

"She squeezed! She squeezed my hand!"

It was at this point in telling the story, that I floundered. My voice trembled as I grasped for words, Luis's hand enveloping mine.

As he kissed them, he asked, "You O.K., hon?"

"Yes...yes," I managed.

How often had I pictured that day and the ones which followed.

Our friends blanched at the image of my traumatized husband bowing under such a burden of sorrow. I stumbled down the hall and into our bedroom where I collapsed, sobbing, onto the bed.

I tried to muffle the sounds. We were, after all, hosting the party. I took a few deep breaths and made an effort to pull myself together.

The other women quietly entered the room. The first wiped the hair from my eyes and mumbled soothing words. The next, joining her, wrapped her arms around me and gently rocked.

The third comforted, "Oh, honey, its O.K. It's over; it's all over now."

I swallowed and shook my head. "You don't understand, but thank you. I think I needed to cry." The memory was fully exposed, finally to be cleansed by tears.

Luis joined us, skirting around our friends. Taking my hand again in his, he drew me safely into his arms.

I was not crying for myself; I was beyond tears. No, I cried for my Luis. He'd come to me in that dark place and cradled my hand in his, just as he was doing now. He was that beacon of light who, with Spirit, inspired me to live.

Blessed, I cried for my love, for his pain and his love for me, and I always will.

EPILOGUE

A message to those who know what it's like To Be Injured

> Control your own destiny or someone else will.
> > Jack Welch

> This above all, to thine own self be true.
> > William Shakespeare

> What are you going to do with your one and precious life?
> > Cheryl Strand

Now, every day when I awaken, I make a choice. I can accept what is expected of me-- that what's lost in being injured, is never restored; what is maintained, never acknowledged. I am caught in a turbulent river of dependence, as my oars lie listless in the hull of my boat. Foaming waters career me, hopelessly, toward the thunderous cascade of despair. If we accept our very identity as "a TBI" (as others define it), we've surrendered before we've even tried. We've chosen to merely "exist," rather than to "live".

When exhausted and feeling you've lost yourself, it may seem easier not to fight it. Why not just succumb and accept what others have said? You are irreparably damaged and in denial about the reality of the situation, to think otherwise.

No, do not give up. Immerse yourself in a creative activity and produce something from your heart. If you love to paint, to refurbish furniture, to draw, to write, to sculpt, to cook, then do it! Through creating something, you will find the Self you thought you'd lost. The form of creative expression may have changed, but these same forces are your heart, your soul, are the very forces which kept you alive. They lie within you, waiting to be recovered so that you, too, can recover. No one can take these away from you, not unless you surrender them.

Through your own recovery, I hope you will try to share your accomplishments with others. Thank you for allowing me the opportunity to try and accomplish that goal for myself.

Yes, you know what it is like To Be Injured. You survived to live fully, and compassionately, the life you've been granted a second time.

About the Author

Carol Gieg grew up in New York and Pennsylvania. She graduated from Dartmouth College, then worked as the assistant manager of a North Face store. She earned a Masters degree in Social Welfare and a Masters in Public Health from the University of California, Berkeley. She has held numerous positions during her 30+ year career, including: psychotherapist in a private practice, case manager with developmentally disabled clients and their families, child therapist with Alameda County, Behavioral Medicine Specialist and Subchief in Santa Rosa, California. She retired as a licensed clinical social worker and now lives in Benicia, California with her husband, Luis.

Made in the USA
Monee, IL
06 September 2023

42267010R00157